# I REGRET
## T H E   D A Y
### I LOST MY VIRGINITY

*YOU ARE NOT YOUR PAST*

# LEANNE LELEE LYONS

### FOREWORD BY MARITA KINNEY

# I REGRET THE DAY I LOST MY VIRGINITY

## YOU ARE NOT YOUR PAST

### LeAnne "LeLee" Lyons
Foreword by Marita Kinney

Pure Thoughts Publishing, LLC

# Copyright

© 2019 by LeAnne "LeLee" Lyons.

All rights reserved. No part of this book may be reproduced, stored in a retrieval system or transmitted in any form or by any means without the prior written permission of the publishers, except by a reviewer who may quote brief passages in a review to be printed in a newspaper, magazine or journal.

All rights reserved.

ISBN: 978-1943409365

Edited by: Diana Owens

Creative Director: Isaac M. Hamm III Make-up Artist: Renee Tucker Stylist: Jumar Edwards Photographer: Nathan Pearcy

Pure Thoughts Publishing, LLC. Conyers, GA 30013

www.purethoughtspublishing.com

Printed in the United States of America.

# DEDICATION

To the woman that gave me life, my mom Margaret Lyons. I was 15 and pregnant with my first child. Of all the anger you had in your heart, you still continued to love me. On the day I went into labor (with the baby girl that would carry your name), you saw the physical pain that my little body was taking. You said to me with tears falling down your face, "Baby if I could take the pain for you I would". That was the mother I had who loved me even in my selfishness. There will never be another you, I miss you so much mommy. RIP

# Acknowledgements

Writing this book was one of the most challenging things I ever had to do. Everything that could go wrong, went wrong, but I kept the faith. I had every reason to believe that my story wasn't supposed to be told, but God restored my mind and gave me the words to say and the strength to push it through.

Showing love to all of who shared my heartache even when I became a headache to them. You must understand that I never forgot what you did for me. (my NYC family, Shareen, Aletha, Tora and Geri Suber, Cassandra, Dana, Kerry Cox, my USI family.)

**Shakim Compere**: I love you to the moon and back. You helped me when no one else would, and I love you for that. I admire you so much in friendship and in business.

**Bishop Orrin Pullings, Sr**: You went beyond the call to help me help a little girl lost. I appreciate you.

**My Pastor Jesse Curney lll**: who always prayed for me and my kids. You always reminded me of my wings to fly.

I'd like to show love to my family, especially my sisters: Jeanette, Sonya, Gigi, Maleia, Latavia, and Bonita. What is a world without sisters? You guys give me the push that I need to move forward.

**T-Roni and Cokonut**: half of this shit you guys already know lol. We have changed music together. We built something great that was life-changing for the three of us. I appreciate all that we have shared together and continue to share. There were some rough waters, but we persevered. I pray that we get as close to the plateau that we deserve. You guys are an inspiration to me, and I love you!

**Laderrick Popeye**): You asked the question, and I gave the answer. From that one conversation we had, I picked up the pen and start writing. You loved the me that that I was never really proud of, and I owe it all to you. You pushed me to my limit, in and out the gym. Together we go far.

To every little girl and young woman, who has a story, and feel like a prisoner in it, let it go! People will always try to control you with something they feel they have over you, but everyone has a story. Be bold in who you are and take the bull by its horns, and always remember that, You are not your past!!! Shine on the world baby!!!!

# CONTENTS

# FOREWORD
## By Marita Kinney, M.MSC

Millions of women can relate to LeAnne's life, as she selflessly shares it with boldness, giving her readers the encouragement to press forward no matter what they have experienced in life. When pain and adversity desperately tried to leave behind shame, hope stepped in providing her strength to overcome all odds. She guides you through the most vulnerable times of her life, leaving her heart on each page.

Life has many twist and turns and it's easy to ignore the difficult journey that our souls had to travel in order to be shaped with stellar character and integrity. Although you sometimes end up with regrets and a chance to redo things, there are blessings and life lessons in each trial. LeAnne chose not to forget about her journey and the lessons that were learned along the way.

At times, overcoming struggles in her life appeared to be impossible, but with faith and perseverance those regrets were turned into some of her most unforgettable accomplishments. Although she has become very successful in her music career, I admire her personal success and determination most.

After meeting with LeAnne, I knew that she had a special story to share. She was telling the story that few people knew, the story of LeAnne. Not LeLee from SWV, but the story that gave her the courage to become a sister with a voice. She's not only sharing her story, but giving women all over the country the courage to overcome their past too. We all have a past, but changing your outlook on it can make a huge difference.

I too had endured many hardships throughout my life and was once haunted by my own regrets. The more I tried to figure things out on my own, the more broken I became. I was addicted to pain and couldn't see myself living any other way. But then something amazing happened. I found my voice and the courage to look at myself differently, realizing that broken crayons still color.

My past became my stepping-stone, giving me the experience to help other hurting people to overcome and redefine their story. With over 58 titles written and published by me, helping hundreds of authors, and determined to aid others in becoming their best self, I now encourage women to see their lives from a victorious point of view much like LeAnne's book. It will allow you the opportunity to discover your courage to move forward too. She's an amazing writer and I can't wait until you read this life changing book.

Marita Kinney, BCC

www.MaritaKinney.com | @marita_lynn_kinney

# INTRODUCTION

I'm LeAnne Lyons, but the world knows me as Lelee, 1/3 of one of the best female R&B trios SWV. I achieved a certain level of success with my singing group selling over 25 million records to date-- but I had bigger problems that started way before then. If you had asked me twenty years ago to put my life and experiences in a book, I'd probably would've told you "hell to the naw". But as life happened for me, I felt compelled to share my story to anyone that would listen. But that didn't happen overnight.

Feeling sorry for myself and not wanting to expose the parties who were involved in the making of my life, I put my dreams as an author--or should I say-- "storyteller" behind me. On the other hand, every opportunity I got to tell my story (e.g. speaking engagements, television, etc.), I found that more and more people were interested in the "old me". It was amazing! For the first time in my life I felt like I mattered. I felt as If I had something other than meaningless sex to offer and a pretty face. In that, I decided I would allow myself to be used again— but this time, I would be the one doing the penetrating. I would penetrate the minds of those that were like me, Feeling ugly, lonely, angry, bitter, and ashamed of their past.

At that point, I realized the worst part of my life was behind me, but my journey didn't stop there. It was right then my moment of epiphany took shape. I had a responsibility to put myself out there as a voice for all little girls and young women all over the world who felt like a prisoner in their own story. I was determined to change that.

From child molestation, evictions, being a teen parent, promiscuity, heartbreak, suicide attempts, death, self-hate, success and homelessness—I was destined to win!

Between my faith in God and my decision to choose life over death—I found my happy place—and that place was always in "ME", I just didn't know it. I allowed myself to give others control of the one thing that I owned-- "ME".

As you read this book, I pray that you experience my journey with an open mind and remove the spirit of judgement. I decided to give my readers the real, raw, and unfiltered me, just the way life was presented to me. I don't know any other way. I appreciate you for wanting to know more about me and I hope that through my dark place, you can find that light at the end of the tunnel.

# Chapter One

## *If It Wasn't for The Bronx*

### (The Boogie down Bronx)

I grew up in the "Highbridge" section of The Boogie Down Bronx. We had a lot of fun growing up as kids--not a worry in the world. We didn't have much of anything, but love was always something that my mother gave us for "Free." She always stressed the importance of love, especially when it came to my siblings and me. Growing up with all girls, my sisters and I would always make the best out of what we had. Although I didn't grow up with a silver spoon in my mouth, I still ate my food with one.

The Boogie Down Bronx (as the locals would call it), most people visiting would probably think of the "Yankees" and the birthplace of Hip-Hop. Although this is true, most of us who lived there knew something a little different. For me, it meant something extraordinary.

When I looked out my window, I heard people talking loud, playing spades in front of the building, local dope boys making a quick sale and drug addicts looking like if they took one more hit, that would be the end. I also saw a fight or two, people arguing over some dumb shit, cigarette butts being flicked on the floor and just locals trying to make the best out of this thing called "life." Oh, let's not forget the rats that were so huge, instead of taking the trash downstairs, you just threw the shit out the window. Those rats would literally take over the garbage cans downstairs, and no one wanted to invade their space--Oh hell no! --Not a rat from NYC.

I had a lot of fun when I was a kid. I was a tomboy, so I did all the cool stuff that the boys did. I climbed trees and gates; especially when we wanted to go to Mullaly pool after hours, we'd have to climb this tall ass gate just to go swimming until we saw a big light flash on us and we got the hell out of dodge. It was the NYPD. We knew we weren't supposed to be in that pool after hours, but we did it anyway. That was just the "Bronx" way, and "OUR" definition of fun.

I also had a lot of fun riding bikes and riding my friends' Big Wheel. See, for those of you who are from the Bronx you know what I'm talking about. The Big Wheel was one of the most popular toys for the boys back in the day. I used to get on that Big Wheel that laid really low, ride it down the ramp and crash it straight into the wall or the gate that was securing a damn near 20 story drop. I promise you, I was supposed to be either dead or broken up real bad because that gate I crashed into was weak as hell. I had no idea why this was so much fun, but it was. I now see why my son is such a daredevil.

For the girly girls: double-dutch, hopscotch, straight rope, and checking out the local boys was some of the fun stuff to do. Yes, the guys back when I was growing up thought they were cool—and they were! If you were a little black girl with thick black hair, you couldn't wait to get your hair straightened. That was the thing to do as a kid. We couldn't wait to see that straightening comb sitting on that hot flame on my mothers' stove. We weren't really into perms in the late seventies, early eighties. That was the style back then just to look really cute. I have a friend who kept her hair laid with that comb. Nobody had better press than her. I remember some of our friends around my way begging her mom to press their hair too. Back then the "mushroom" hairdo was fashionable. If you can imagine one big bang going around your whole head like a headband--this was considered a mushroom.

My sisters and I had fairly good hair that would have a little wave to it when it got wet. My mom straightened me and my sisters' hair, but it was not as straight as my friend Allandra's lol. I never understood what her moms' secret was until my mother discovered "DAX" hair straightening grease. This damn grease was strong, thick, and smelled like something a doctor would give you to put on an injured foot. Nevertheless, who cared—?

That was the secret to a good ole hair straightening.

## My School Years

We were living on Anderson Avenue in the Bronx when I started my first day of Kindergarten. I can't remember everything that happened—not that my life was that damn exciting at five years old--, but what I do recall, it was a lot of fun. Mrs. Hand was my favorite teacher of all time. There was really nothing special about this Caucasian woman with long straight brown hair, who was reminiscent of Laura Ingalls from "Little House on The Prairie." I have no idea what the obsession was, but she was the sweetest person in the world. Yeah, that was it!

Mrs. Hand would always come to class with a TAB soda that she would never finish. I can remember being thirsty as hell every time she clicked that damn soda open. I don't know, I guess I just wanted to know what that shit tasted like. The funny thing is, I would eventually become a teenager, a young adult, and finally a grown-ass woman-- and still--til this day, I don't know what that hell that TAB soda tastes like.

As the years went by, I was really starting to grow up. I was now in the first grade and hated every minute of it! Lord, please forgive me, but I had the ugliest, meanest teacher in the world. Her name was Mrs. Bowles. I get annoyed, even mentioning her name, and to know this lady was married shocks the hell out of me. Her husband back then must've been blind, crippled, and damn crazy to deal with a nutcase like her. No exaggeration, Mrs. Bowles was like a slimmer version of Madea! She barely yelled, but used this wicked witch type voice to reprimand you-- and it was very intimidating. I'll never

4

forget as long as I live when we had a PTA meeting (Parents and Teachers Association). For some reason, my mother couldn't make it, so my dad came. I knew I was in for something.

The two of them together was like Satan himself just met his best friend. Long story short, she told my dad that I was way too talkative in the class and I hummed a lot, which was a disturbance to the other 1st graders. Disturb them from what? Tracing a damn L on the dots? Well anyway, by the end of this, my father gave this witch permission to spank me in front of the whole class.

I couldn't believe it! The damn ruler was taller than me and thick as hell. I promise you, I wanted both of them to walk in the street on the Grand Concourse (a high traffic area in the Bronx, NY) holding hands and walk right in front of traffic. Although I don't think I deserved this at all, this is what I had to deal with. I think I started to develop some hate towards my father at this point. Who would allow a teacher to spank their kid in front of the whole class and be embarrassed? She'd sit in a chair directly in front of the chalkboard, have me get the ruler (which was bigger than me) and have me lay over her knee on my stomach as if I was in a plank position. Well, she spanked my ass every chance she got. If I stayed in the bathroom too long, if I was out of the line, etc., it was a hot mess. Half my class thought it was funny, and the other half was afraid they would be next on her ass whipping list.

She traumatized me, and from this experience alone, I'll grow up with very little confidence, thinking every time I went in front of people, they were laughing at me and not with me. I found out later that Mrs. Bowles would later on yell and say the wrong things to a kid and was fired from her teaching position. God don't like ugly!

One thing I did love about school was auditorium time when we would put on shows and watch movies. My favorite film in elementary school was "The Red Balloon." It was a movie about a young boy who couldn't live without his red balloons, which turned into a hot air balloon whenever he would dream about something, or someplace, he wanted to go. It was like magic. And every time he'd fulfill one of his dreams, one of his balloons would pop when he came back to reality. I wanted to borrow his balloons so bad. While all the other kids were talking, I meshed into this movie as a young girl. I guess it's safe to say I was a dreamer even at five and six years old.

The teachers would allow us to bring a snack to school to eat at snack time. Kids brought everything from Wise cheese doodles, onion rings, barbeque chips, and sometimes fresh fruit. Unfortunately, I didn't always have the luxury of bringing a snack to school every day, so sometimes I would just sit there and feel my nose just scan the foods on each of my classmates' desk. In my head, I could taste the cheese and the barbeque on my tongue. A few of the kids would tease me for not having anything to eat at "snack time." I would ask to be excused and go to the bathroom and just cry.

I felt so bad for myself, but I would quickly get myself together. I wouldn't dare go back in that classroom crying like a baby. One day, I just got sick of being the girl that got laughed at, you know, the standout girl. I got so sick of being made fun of about something I had no control over. Sometimes I forgot to bring a snack and other times we just couldn't afford it. So, one day, I didn't have a snack to eat, so I did the unthinkable and stole my classmate's apple out of her desk. She was a white girl named Annie. I remember that day so bright. She was looking for her snack in tears, and here I go busting out with a fresh red delicious apple sitting at my desk like it was mine. Even at that age, I wasn't a good thief because I literally sat right next to the girl I just robbed lol. It was the most obvious and embarrassing thing in the world. She went to the teacher and told her that she believed I stole her apple, and my teacher called me up to the desk. You would think I would have gone up there alone, knowing I just did some foul shit, but not LeAnne. Not only did my dumb ass take the apple with me, but I had just taken the biggest bite out of it. All the evidence was in my mouth.

"LeAnne, did you bring a snack to school this morning, because Annie is missing her apple"? "LeAnne, did you do something you were not supposed to do"? "Yes," I said. She asked me again, "LeAnne, did you bring a snack to school this morning"? Starting to cry, I said, "No." "Did you take Annie's apple"? Yes, I said. "I think you owe her an apology and another apple. She went on to explain to me because of my wrongdoing, now my mother was responsible for replacing it. Of course, she called my mom, and I was in a lot of trouble, which I should have been. My mother ended up buying Annie a few apples, and I had to have a quiet snack time for five school days. Shit, that was the last time I stole something from anybody. It would end up biting me in the ass because I would end up spending thousands of dollars fixing shit my kids did that, I had nothing to do with. What a great lesson to learn.

I used this experience as motivation to get me through my next couple of years in elementary school the right way. I wasn't a harmful or disrespectful kid, I just did dumb shit every now and then, just like any other kid—at least that's what I thought. This is the moment I realized that all kids don't do wrong.

As far as I can remember, I've always wanted to be good at something, not quite an over-achiever, but just wanted to be acknowledged for something good that I've done. As a little girl, I remember being in elementary school craving attention from my teachers. I wanted to be the one that was called on to be the class monitor. The class monitor was chosen to do every damn thing: the line leader, paper assignment handler, etc. He/she wasn't just any student—he/she was an exceptional student. You had to really be on top of your game to be considered for this particular assignment. My favorite was being able to privately eat lunch in the classroom with the teacher at lunchtime.

When I reached the fourth grade, there were two Spanish girls in my class who could do no wrong in any teachers' eyes—Kathy and Carlina. Kathy was a tall model height girl who wore glasses and her hair in a thick ponytail braid. Unlike Kathy, Carlina was a short girl with the prettiest, thickest short, curly hair who also wore glasses. I don't know, but there is something special about people who wear glasses. "The Awesome Two," as I called them, were who you would consider the "model" students in our school. They were respectful, very well versed, and never got in any kind of trouble. I think they were the first ones at school all the time, and the last ones to leave. They studied, studied, studied, and volunteered as much as they could all while maintaining an "A" average. Shit, I wanted to be a part of that life.

There was no one in the school they could compete with, but each other. Those two would get picked to do almost everything in the world, and I can honestly say they delivered. They were just good at every damn thing. Whenever we would have a school play, they both had leading roles, they were picked as class monitors for the Kindergarten classes, and they were chosen to be the paper monitors, amongst other things. The paper monitor was just the girl who gave out the assignments for the day with that beautiful smell of "new ink." With everything going on in the family life that I couldn't control, I just wanted to do something that not only made my parents proud, but made myself proud too. Instead of me being consumed with everything that was going on with all the other kids, I was trying to figure out how I could be friends with the teachers' pets—Kathy and Carlina.

I figured the only way I could get people to notice me was to do something that everybody couldn't do—sing. I tried out for one of the History plays and was picked to sing, "O Danny Boy," and "The Autumn Leaves" in the assembly. Not only was I excited, but my plan actually worked. It was the gift that attracted the "Awesome Two" so much that they instantly began talking to me and congratulating me. The next day I felt awesome that everything worked out. The "Awesome Two" began conversing with me, which is when I quickly noticed how most of their conversation was about school and books. At this point, that was cool with me because I had two new friends. Not just any two friends, I was friends with the smartest kids in the school. I have to be honest, after getting to know them, I was so much more focused on the right things. My school life instantly changed from getting my ass kicked from Mrs. Bowles, to eating lunch in the classroom with my teacher and the "Awesome Two." It was then they recognized another one of my gifts, which attracted them to me even more. My penmanship and my ability to write well sealed the deal for me. Everything was smooth sailing after that.

## Middle School

Diana Sands JHS 147 was the middle school me and my sister Jeanette went to. It was there that I realized what I wanted to do professionally and honed my skills. Although I was a timid kid (at least at some things), I still tried to participate in most of the events they had going on at the school. I think I tried damn near everything: the chorus, talent shows, and I even took a chance playing the clarinet. I hate that damn instrument to this day. I don't know why it just didn't have enough soul in it I guess lol.

It was JHS that I met my first real love, Robert, aka Topsport. Robert was one of the cutest guys in the school, and he could dance his ass off. He had height, looks, and moves lol. I thought he would be the guy that I marry one day. Well, come on, I wasn't thinking back then at all, I was twelve give me a break. I remember whenever we'd have talent shows Rob would dance to Michael Jackson. I was so hooked on this guy that whenever he would bust a move, I thought Michael was in the room. Rob liked me, but he had a wandering eye, even at our age. I'd never forgotten the days I use to walk Rob home (I had to walk by his building to go to my house), he would give me a kiss, and I thought I was going to die. One thing I noticed was he would always rush and close the door after the quick kiss. I didn't understand then, but I sure get it now. Rob was also crushing on one of the local Spanish girls in the community. For those of you who are not familiar with the Puerto Rican boo thangs in the Bronx—They're hot!! This girl had everything he loved that I couldn't buy at the corner store if I wanted to—tits and lots of ass—yes even at that age. Oh well, the funny part is I would go into my adult life with insecurities about my body. That's another chapter.

## Walton High School

After getting rejected by the high school that I really wanted to go to (Fiorello LaGuardia High School), which was THEE performing arts high school to go to if you wanted to be somebody in the entertainment industry, I decided to go to Walton High School in the Bronx. I thought I did an excellent job at the audition, but I didn't meet the academic requirements needed to move forward. I wasn't that great in science and missed the criteria required by a few points because I was so tired and didn't study for that test. Shit had I known that the one time I tried to beat the system would eventually bite me in the ass and cost me my dream high school, I would've stayed up all night to make that happen. I must admit, I was mad as hell at myself for a while about this, but I had to do what I had to do.

And on the other hand, it taught this middle schooler a lifelong lesson—stay ready, so you won't have to get ready. I mean, who wouldn't want to have gone to the school that trained some of the greats in entertainment today. Stars like Alicia Keys, Lauren Hill, Marlon Wayans, Omar Epps, all were alumni of this great existence.

High School was ok. At this time, I guess we were living with my Godmother Jet after getting evicted. Living in a one-bedroom apartment with five people wasn't that much fun at all, but somehow, we made it work. There was always some kind of distraction when I was in high school. I remember being in my homeroom class, and as we sat there waiting to take attendance, a shoe would come flying through the window from the hallway into the classroom. Me being me, I always thought the shit was funny especially if it hit someone and didn't hurt them really bad lol. This would happen all the time, especially when we'd be taking tests. Whoever was doing this, he/she would wait good and ready for the classroom to be quiet. After a while, it wasn't funny anymore, it became more of a distraction. That didn't work for me at all.

Being at what was considered one of the worst high schools in NYC, academically I was doing well. Of course, like everybody else, I sort of struggled in Social Studies and Math a little bit, but it wasn't as bad as you may think. I always ended up passing with a C. For some reason, it was still those two classes that was a mess. I played Basketball for a few semesters until I got elbowed really bad, and it was then I realized that it wasn't for me. I figured I'd be better in chorus—and I was right.

Chorus was so much fun! There was a girl in my class named Jenny that could sing so well. I can still remember the tone of her voice and how she wasn't afraid to reach vocally. Our teacher would play a chord on the piano or give her a note, and she'd go for it, even if it hurt. It was almost like we weren't even there. She wasn't afraid to mess up and had confidence out the roof, but was very humble as well. I really wish I could've adapted that confidence from Jenny in ninth grade—I'd be so much further in life right now and my career would've been through the roof. I just never liked attention on me, whether good or bad. I know it's crazy as hell, but that was little ole me.

I used to always hook up with my friend Keneesha Gill who was also in my chorus class. Her parents were in the church and very religious, so all she really listened to was gospel songs. One song that I always loved was, "We come this far by Faith." She and I used to walk through the halls, harmonizing the chorus to that song every time the bell rang. We'd get everyone's attention singing through the hall on our way to our next class. I have to say that she's probably the first person who really knew I could really sing beside my cousin Tasheva. On another note, I recruited her to be a member of my group at the time, but her mom wanted her to stay in the church and focus on school-- which was a good choice. Not a lot of people know that story.

# CHAPTER TWO

## *I Got Jumped*

I was a thirteen-year-old hanging out with my older cousin Jennifer in the Bronx. In the hood when you grow up closely with someone, you address them as, "my cousin", "my Aunt", etc. Everyone was family whether biologically or part of your extended family. She was almost three years older than me and boy did we hang out tough. Jen was one of those really skinny girls with a real big mouth but will back her shit up in a heartbeat. That girl would fight anyone who wanted smoke and sometimes they didn't have to bring it to her—she'd bring it to them. Don't get me wrong, she wasn't that bad that she couldn't get her ass kicked but backing down wasn't going to happen. Now that I think of it, all of my good fighting, I did with Jennifer lol.

I have to tell this story now that I'm thinking of it. I was, I guess its safe to say "liking" because shit I was too young to say "dating" this guy named Omar. I knew Omar from the church I was going to. When I tell you, I was liking this boy so much

I was so upset that he started liking this Spanish girl named "Diana". Diana was a cute little spanish girl with buck teeth. Not so buck that it made her unattractive, because she was still cute. We were talking for a few months and just like a young boy, he did his share of spreading his wings.

Anyway, I was so distraught about this and my cousin caught wind of it. Somehow, the new girlfriend and I exchanged words and she was talking some real heavy shit. Of course, back when we were kids, we were very petty, and we were emotional and would fight over dudes. I refuse to get over the fact that he dumped me for another girl. Not only that, but he would lie about it, not knowing she already told me. She would answer his phone and everything when I called him. So, one day, we decided we'd just take a walk past her building down the stairs on Anderson and 166th Street. All we wanted to do was see if he was on her block and catch him in a damn lie. Chile, when we got down the steps, we saw her in front of her building with her family. Now keep in mind, it was only me and Jennifer together when there were about six people in front of her building. I told my cousin, "that's her". She walked up to her and asked, "Is your name Diana?". In a stink, nasty, Spanish tone, she replied, "Why?", I could've taken her head and banged it somewhere. I'm like, do this chick know who she's talking too. My cousin is cookoo for coco puffs. Here go Jennifer's ass, "Bitch cuz I wanna know". OMG!!!! All I could think of was the 6:2 ratio between us and her family. There was a good chance they'll probably take us down, but shit we were bold as hell. I had to side with my cousin even if she was wrong, but I have to say Diana opened that door. After her smart-ass remark, my cousin yelled, "Fuck her up LeAnne". I'm like "Oh shit". Now, you hear them talking amongst each other in Spanish so all we could do is feel everything out. It was starting to be obvious that a commotion was going on. We were going back and forth with each other cussing and yelling. I think her people was telling her to whip my ass because she squared up with me. That's all I had to see before I wore that bitch out. She was cute and all, but that chic couldn't fight to save her life. "Beat her ass", my cousin yelled, while her family was probably yelling something similar to her in Spanish. We were thumping for real in front of her building, around her family. I wasn't sure how this was going to play out but all I knew was I was whipping her ass. I caught her around a tree punching her in the face and I guess I got her in a position where she was stuck. She kept trying to hit me but had her in an awkward position, so basically the fight was over. I was stuck to that bitch like a dog getting a good piece of ass. When my cousin pulled me from her, that girls face was so red and swollen. I kinda felt bad because I knew we didn't really come to do that, we were trying to catch ole boy in a lie, that's all.

When we ran back up the steps, my cousin and I was assessing my body to see if she probably had gotten a hit that we missed. Well, the only thing we noticed was a cut-like bruise on my left hand. She dug her nail really deep in my skin and it opened me up a little. It took that damn thing forever to heal, in fact, I still see it in my hand today almost thirty-four years later.

Even though Jen wasn't exactly the best influence on me, I could always count on her when shit hit the fan. I don't know if it was me, but it seemed like everyone either wanted to fight her, or was afraid to fight her. With her very slim stature, if you didn't know her, you would definitely sleep on her.

## I GOT JUMPED

One thing about New York honey, nobody fights fair. You're going to either get shanked, stabbed, or jumped by a gang of chicks. This story wasn't any different for me. Another incident was when I was walking to my Godmother Jet's house from where my mother lived on 174th Street and Grand Concourse. One thing about New Yorkers, we do way more walking than driving, and those who have a car they weren't driving it or didn't have no damn insurance. In my case, I was too young to have a car and at that time, if I was of age, I probably couldn't afford one anyway—so walking was our thing. Still kinda liking Omar, I would purposely walk past his block, hoping he and his brothers would be outside so he could see how cute I looked. Sometimes I was successful, other times I wasn't, but this particular day no one was outside, so I kept going. As I passed this park on Summit Avenue, there were a few guys hanging out playing ball. So, as I walked past the basketball court, a few guys were whistling at me. Initially, I ignored it because I'm not a damn dog, and even back then,

I didn't respond to boys whistling at me. I could hear the guys whispering about who was going to approach me. Lo and behold, as I kept walking, the shortest one out the crew thought he'd take his shot. He was a half cute dude, just short as hell. He caught up with me giving me a few feet asking me my name—I told him. "You a cutie, can I call you sometimes?", he said. I politely said, "No". "Why?", he said. "No offense, but you're way too short for me. You're a cutie but just too short."

If looks could kill, that lil black nigga turned red in the face. Suddenly, I wasn't the cute girl anymore and he damn sure didn't want my number now. As his friends witnessed his rejection, he started to get really pissed off and insult me. "Fuck you bitch', he said. "I didn't want ya wack ass anyway, I just wanted to fuck you". I looked at him and said, "Get your gorilla looking ass out my face, fuck you little boy". It was just terrible. It got so bad that people started to come outside, look out their windows and everything. It even brought some of his family members outside who then started their own beef with me. As I got closer to my Godmother's house, I started to see people I knew so he kinda fell back. Then his sister who was just as short, but had a big ass mouth said, "I'm gon fuck you up bitch fucking with my brother". "Bitch you can get it too," I said. Some people I knew, and some of my sisters' friends asked me what was wrong, and I told them. They said leave that shit alone, and I did. I had gotten to my destination and started doing other shit. About an hour later, someone that knew me and the guy that started with me heard about the confrontation and said they were heated. I'm like for what? He started with me first and then his sister got in it. I honestly couldn't understand why he took everything so serious, but we had to figure this thing out. My main concern was how mad was he? Damn, I'm starting to believe the rejection in front of his friends got the best of him, and he couldn't deal with it. Anyhow, my friend said the guy's sister wanted a one on one with me. I said, "fuck it", cool.

At this point my adrenaline was on ten. I was so sick of him and his damn sister. This dude had initiated a fight between his sister and I, and it was to take place that evening on their block. This was the dumbest thing ever to me. They were arranging a fight as if we were getting paid for it or something. But what the hell, we were all very immature twelve and thirteen-year olds. At this point, the whole block heard about it and everyone wanted to get involved. So, what started as a small argument, then went to a fight between me and someone that had nothing to do with it and ended up being what felt like a damn turf war. The whole damn block was ready and hot—at least that's what we thought.

So, the time came for us to go to the dude's block and it was almost dark outside. I can't front, I was nervous as hell because for one, I had no idea what would be waiting on the other side, and two, we were dumb as hell for agreeing to fight someone on their block.

## THE PULL UP

As me, Jen and about twenty-five to thirty people from my block approached Merriam Avenue, it looked like a straight up war zone. they came to kick our asses. Surrounding them were pit bulls, sticks, thugs, and the girls they had were huge man looking chicks. Of course, me and Jennifer was leading the pack and when we saw what was going down, we made it clear that it was going to be a one on one fight between the girl and I. "NO JUMPING", one of the dudes from my block said. I'm nervous as hell, my body all of a sudden felt limp, but my adrenaline was at one hundred. I was an emotional wreck for real. All I could think of was how I was going to get the best of this bitch and come out alive.

As we got closer, I could hear the guy Sean say, "that's that bitch right there". As I looked, I'm like, whoahhhh!!! This is not even the girl I was there to fight. They got some other chick to fight me. Oh well, no time to pussy around now. I wanted to get this thing over, so they spread out and the bitch came out of nowhere, swung on me and missed. She was short too, so her reach was very weak—but mines wasn't. When she missed me and I caught her, all I know is I see this big man looking chic come towards me and swing. She caught me on my side. At this time, we backed into a parked car. I pulled her towards me so I can use her as cover to cover to block the big chic from hitting me. I hear lots of screaming from both sides. My block telling me to "Kick her ass", all the while Jennifer was swinging on any and everybody because at this time, everybody realized I was getting jumped. Basically, everybody was swinging and things got out of hand for real. As one of the girls I was fighting friends pulled her from me, all I can feel was a punch here, a punch there. I buckled up my body so I could take the hits, but I was blocking my face at the same time. Like a raging bull, I had a clear shot of the big chick when I got up from the car, POW!!! I punched her in the face and that shocked everybody. "I got the biggest bitch", I thought., so I was good. I had a clean shot and must have hit her pretty hard because she was pretty much done. Egging me on, I could here Jennifer saying, "Fuck that Bitch Up", her famous line. Making sure everything was clear, I'm wondering why it got so quiet on our side. What started off as twenty-five and thirty people ended up being only four of us. All them pretty bitches talking all that shit on my block was GONE. It was said to me that when they saw I was getting jumped and everybody was swinging they left.

The cops were called, and the fight was over! Suddenly, everything on the opponents' end calmed down. They spread out and left one by one, dog by dog. In the end, it was only me and Jennifer left to fend for ourselves, and like always, we ended up doing just that. People from the opponents' side was walking up to us saying how we tore they asses up and they couldn't believe how I took the biggest chic. I didn't care what he was saying, I just wanted some water and to get home. I was dehydrated and mad as hell at them so called friends who left me for dead pretty much. I never depended on anyone to fight for me since then.

# CHAPTER THREE

## The Gift of Song

M usic didn't only save my life, but it made my life. Ever since I could remember the gift of song was in my belly. My mom tried putting me in so many things, but the music was always a hit with me. Growing up around mostly adults who had an ear for the best music that was out at that time, I developed this love for the music my parents used to listen to around the house first: Blues, R&B and Jazz.

With no formal training at all, my mother was a naturally gifted musician. She played piano by ear. I wasn't sure where the musical influence came from in her family, until a few years ago. I met some of my extended family on her side and was surprised to find out they were filled with preachers and singers for real. Chile, the singing my cousins were doing made my whole heart happy.

Music was a must in our house. Between the vinyl records, my parents would play, the eight-track tapes, or the piano we had that sat against the wall until mom decided she wanted to play, there was music everywhere in my house. It wasn't all the time that the piano got beat on, but when it did, it was a great moment for our family. We automatically knew it was time to stop whatever the hell we were doing and get in singing mode. You would've thought we were a community choir getting paid for a gig as loud as we were clapping and singing.

When we gathered around the piano, Mommy would play these Bluesy chords before she would start to sing this one gospel song by the Pilgrim Travelers called "When I Should Feel So Sad." The song sounded like one of those sad funeral songs, but it was surprisingly a positive song. We would all sing the lyrics loud and proud:

When I should feel so sad

Why does my soul feel so glad

Why does my heart feel so happy and gay

When all around me burdens roll

Yet I'm not worried at all

For when I pray, King Jesus will roll my burdens away...

This was one of the oldest songs known to man but had significant meaning in my mother's life. So, for her to share it with us was epic. Today, gospel fans are more into more contemporary Gospel music, but every now and then, my sisters and I would still hum a verse or two of my mother's favorite hymns.

Although my mom didn't raise us in the church, it was obvious that she had her own personal relationship with God. She would frequently quote scriptures from the bible to us that we didn't realize were scriptures until we became Christians ourselves as adults. So, her faith was strong, even up until the day she passed away.

## The Dirty South

Many don't know this because I spend so much time with my sisters, but I do have a brother as well. My brother was my mother's first-born child, and she loved him to pieces. The girls being born and raised in New York City, and he in the South, the only time I got to see him was when we made summer visits to Atlanta. My brother was old enough to be my father, and we have many years between us. Therefore, the closeness I shared with my sisters was pretty much non-existent with him. Don't get me wrong, I knew I had a brother because my mom told me, and I've spent many summers living with him, but for some reason, I never felt that brother/sister connection with him that I felt with my sisters. I hate that our relationship, even til this day, is estranged. I always longed for that big brother/ little sister bond, but it was always a struggle. But most surprisingly, I had a connection with him that I didn't have with my sisters, and that was musical—my brother can sho nuff sing.

When I think of my brother's singing voice, I'm quickly reminded of Sam Cooke. I always enjoyed when he sang R&B songs on the radio, but when he sang those quartet style gospel songs, he had my full attention. My brother would drive the hell out of a gospel song in full voice for a whole fifteen, twenty minutes a song—and do it with his entire body soaking wet and his face, forget about it. It's hard for a professional singer to sing for four whole minutes sometimes, depending on the song, but this was the most impressive thing I had ever seen, especially in a non-professional setting. I don't care what anyone says, he was professional in my eyes.

I got to hear my brother sing all the time. I was a little kid mesmerized every time he opened his mouth to sing a note. He was a straight-up beast when it came to performing, and I soaked it up every time. I would watch, learn, take notes, and put every single moment in my long-term memory bank. From the way he walked on the stage, addressed the crowd, and his showmanship and presence on stage was everything. That's one connection I will forever have with my brother.

My Aunt Regina's husband, Uncle Bobby was very influential musically in my life. He played the electric guitar and would always take time showing me different chords to play. He was also a singer in his own right. His voice had that grit in it that only preachers could pull off. You know that squally kind of voice. There was one song that he would listen to by gospel legends the Mighty Clouds of Joy called "Moving on Up." I could tell every time he heard this song, he got happy. He would grab his guitar and go into this jam session, just him, and the Mighty Clouds of Joy cd. If I were not playing outside or trying to sneak to the candy lady's house, I would always join uncle B. "Come on Over Here," he would say. I would sit next to him, and he would break the harmonies up in parts. "Sing this," he said, and he went straight to his guitar. Uncle Bobby was the first person I ever heard harmonize. I had no idea what harmonizing was until he told me. He would teach me the line in the song "Movin on Up...." and as I sang the main note, he too would chime in. It was so good I wanted to do it over and over again. It was also where I first heard the song "Flashlight" by Parliament. I miss my Uncle Bobby so much.

When it came to tone, my other Godmother Johnella Hall (singer Aaron Hall's mother) taught me all about it. When I tell you, her little self had the most beautiful tone ever, please believe me. I could hear her singing now as she would put her hand over her mouth in a shy manner. She would so beautifully start to sing and teach me the gospel song "Love Lifted Me." Jonella's tone was a mix between Brandy and Lalah Hathaway all in one. I could hear her singing in my ear right now.

She and I would harmonize so well together, and whenever I would get pitchy, she had no problem telling me. "No baby girl, you're not listening," she'd say. "The same way you hear me talk to you is the same way you have to listen to melodies and notes," she would always say. Now her sister Rozelia, another singer in her own right, with a beautiful tone as well, was the strict one when you would fuck up your notes. I believe she was trying to make my sisters and I a group as much as she had us singing. Whenever we were together, the Pointer Sisters song, "He so shy." She would have us in a line singing in harmony,

"He's so shy"......

"He's so shy

That sweet little boy

Who caught my eye.

## The Artists

It was nothing for you to come to my house any day of the week and hear the sounds of some of the hottest artists out at that time. My father was so cheap he never bought anything but the newspaper every day, so he took full advantage of the music that played on the radio. My mother, being from the South, really embraced many of the southern artists at that time. One record she would have in heavy rotation was a singer from Memphis, Tennessee named Bobby Blue Bland. Bobby Blue Bland was a crooner with one of the sexiest tones in the business. His voice was so distinctive, you automatically knew one of his songs when you heard it. He had all the ladies going crazy—and the kids too. Ruth Brown was one of my mother's favorite artists. Mom used to play one of her live CDs, and there was a song called, "Mama, He Treats Your Daughter Mean," that I used to love so much, especially the Live version.

There was something about the instrumentation in the songs that I loved, especially the horns.

But there was always one Queen that I enjoyed that I continue to listen to til this day, and that's Ms. Millie Jackson. Mommy would secretly play this record because of its risqué content. I wasn't sure what the contents were suggesting, but I sure know that she was loud, bold, and a good cusser. Millie Jackson was hands down one of my favorite people to listen to and watch perform. I was a little kid at the time and had no business listening to these records, but they were funky, soulful, and full of shit-talking comedy. It was the first time I heard someone say "Fuck" in a song, and it sounded so good to me. While my mom would hide these records, I happen to find the album cover one day behind this stereo system and decided I would try to figure out what the contents were on this sexy ass record. It was the record with Millie sitting on the toilet seat—a classic album still today. But hands down, it was the Millie Jackson "Uncensored" record with my favorite album cut to this day, "I Had to Say It" that shaped my whole persona. Ms. Millie was Lil Kim before Lil Kim was Lil Kim. There was no artist, especially a female artist that was comfortable talking shit like Millie Jackson. She was bold, confident, and gritty with it. She was one of the artists that wasn't afraid to be free, and I enjoyed every minute of it. Let's just say that the Queen of shit talking was the inspiration for most things Lelee that the world knows. I'm a proud cusser and professional shit talker today, but no one would ever do it like the Queen Millie.

It wasn't just Miss Millie, I believe it was the era in which a lot of these artists came out. Unlike many of today's performers, back then people went through some real grown people shit, and musicians weren't afraid to sing about it. One artist would talk about how he wanted to have sex with someone else's woman, while the other one talked about what she's going to do to your ass if that ever happens to her. Whatever the case, it was the kind of stories that many, especially in the hood, had a connection with. This kind of behavior was going on right in our own backyard, and we wrote about it.

By connecting with this music and the artists of this era, I can see a lot of my personality in it for sure. I've been through a lot personally, and just like these records, I was never afraid to talk about it. When you're comfortable speaking of the very things that make people uncomfortable, you'll always win. People can see through the fake shit.

## The Music

I realized I could sing at about six or seven years old. I would be in school singing so much that I got in so much trouble for it. I knew then that, just because I wanted to hear me, it didn't mean everyone else felt the same way. In a weird kind of way, that's how I felt damn near my whole career in the music business. At home, I would play the "Dreamgirls" album so much that the record would start to skip. Back then, my voice was much higher than it is now, and I would sing those songs in full voice. I used to stand and sing so loud in my house that all I could hear my sisters say to me was, "Shut up that noise, that's not singing that's screaming." I didn't give a damn, whenever one of my favorite singers came on the radio, especially Stephanie Mills, I would try so hard to sing like her but couldn't. Stephanie had one of the most recognizable voices in the business then, and now, and she had this vibrato that only someone with that "special throat" could do. It was so fast and controlled, and I loved every minute of it. I could not understand how someone so little can have so much power in their voice. From "Sweet Sensation," to "Never Knew Love Like This Before," to one of my favorite vocal performances by her to date," I Feel Good." This song was one of my favorites, but came out at a time when my dad left his family for another woman. He and his new lady friend danced to this song at our family reunion, while my mom sat in that room, and watched with so much class. I hate that now I must associate one of my favorite songs with a bittersweet time in my life, but it was at that moment I realized the gift of song.

Deniece Williams was also one of the artists that I loved growing up as a kid. In fact, on my eleventh birthday, with my birthday money, all I wanted was the "Black Butterfly" 45 single from the record store and to see the movie Purple Rain. See, I was a different kind of kid. While all the kids my age was racing to the store to buy candy or waiting to hear the "Mister Softee" ice-cream truck, I was buying records with my money. I think my world in entertainment was starting to birth at that very moment. "Let's Hear It for the Boy" was on the flip side of the "Black Butterfly" single. That was the song that made me so happy and jumpy. I'd find myself imitating Deniece in the mirror as I held my brush in my hand as a microphone and start singing my heart out. While back then, I didn't focus much on the lyrics in a song, today that song has a special meaning because Lord knows I have dated the regular guy that wasn't popular—but he was special to me.

It wasn't until my very first concert ever that I realized what I wanted to do one day. My father surprised me and my sister Jeanette with tickets to see a young singer that I would cry about, and her name was Stacy Lattisaw. Stacy was one of the youngest, successful artists out at that time with the biggest voice I ever heard coming from a little girl. Watching her perform was such a treat, but on stage, she came across really shy—almost looking like she didn't want to be there. But, she looked beautiful, and you could tell she loved to sing. She had a song out at that time called "Miracles," "Love on a Two-Way Street," and the fun song "Attack of the Name Game." You couldn't tell me shit when I sang these songs. I just loved Stacy and would've loved to see her more in concert.

A song wasn't just a song to me. It was three or four minutes of someone's life experience —good, bad, or ugly. Music had the power to break up relationships or put one back together. It was that word processor that we needed at the time when we just couldn't find the right words to say to someone we loved. There were really only two kinds of music that did that for me, and that was that gritty, R&B Soul, and the good ole down home Blues. Don't get me wrong, I enjoyed a lot of the pop songs out at that time as well; Phil Collins, Barbra Streisand, Janis Joplin, and damn near all the artists who were on some kind of drug had a special place in my heart, whether prescribed drugs, or from the street—they were some talented people.

Ever since I can remember, I've always been a lover of old school music. Most of my favorite artists today are either deceased or on their way. On Rhythm and Blues, I can go on and on naming the great artists who made this dream of mine all possible.

## The Dream

Coming home from shooting our first music video "Right Here" was so exciting and tiring at the same time. My family still didn't have a place of our own and were still staying at my Godmother's one-bedroom apartment in the Bronx. I was exhausted with the scene changes, getting makeup done, and just the beating that came with being up for fourteen hours straight with no rest. I couldn't believe there was a possibility that my life could change in just a few months.

I remember being dropped off in front of my building around 3a.m. in the morning, and of course the block was HOT. It was mid-summer, and everyone was congregated in front of the building. Here I am, getting out of my Lincoln Town Car with full glam, and an overnight bag with a few of the clothes we were able to keep from the video shoot. As usual, I'd walk up towards my neighbors to say, "what's up", and here goes my friend Chance, "Why you got all that makeup on?" I smiled and said, "I just did a video". "A video for what", he said. "For my song with my singing group."

Of course, he thought it was funny as hell. Everyone on the block knew I could sing because they'd always ask me to sing, "Who Holds Tomorrow" in the hallway when it was raining outside. I gladly accepted because the acoustics in that building was so pretty. It made me sound like I was in Carnegie Hall. I guess there's always a little doubt as the dream gets closer to reality, but it felt great just knowing I was doing something that I loved, that could possibly change me and my kids' lives. This was really happening y'all.

The first time I heard our first single on the radio, we were in Los Angeles about to begin the first leg of our promo tour for our debut album, "It's About Time". We were in the limo on our way to the hotel and we damn near went bananas. That's Us, That's Us!! We were screaming all over the place with excitement. I think the driver closed the partition because we were so loud. If you would have asked the little girl in me, what she wanted to do when she got older, she probably would've told you be a mortician. Never in a million years would I have ever imagined that God would bless me with opportunities that I probably didn't deserve. For that I am forever grateful.

It would be a long time before I ever got that excited about anything in my life again. To be exact, that day would come in the year 2014 when my grandbaby was born. After all of my lessons and disappointments, she gave me the will to want to live again—on purpose. I knew when she smiled at me and my heart would just melt that I had to continue on dreaming. I had to keep on living so that she could live a good life, and that's a feeling I will never forget.

For the first time I knew what true love felt like. I'm not sure what the hell I was doing in all these other relationships that kept me crying my eyes out and taking me on an emotional roller coaster all these years, but clearly it never felt like this. Going through my evictions and instabilities, I believed that money would change all of these things, and for a minute, it did. But when you're making more money than the average person you have a whole new set of problems. Now, you're able to sleep good at night, but you never wake up happy.

Although, I never felt like one, I thought being a so-called celebrity, and being a part of a successful brand would be the end of my problems, at least that's what I was told. But in fact, this was the period where I was the unhappiest. I never felt good enough, I never felt accomplished, I definitely didn't feel successful. To me, anything that was considered successful didn't feel like a failure. My dream had me surrounded by many people who didn't think I was great at pretty much anything, but never took the time to show me how to get there. I know you're probably thinking, "Girl you guys sold millions and millions of records, how could you say that". Yes, that we did, but technically our label was successful, the writers and producers were successful, but I never felt that we were. All the years of hard work that it took to pull off what we've done, I don't have anything but dusty plaques and memories to show for it—but this was still my dream.

The dream had me feeling like I was in the sunken place and couldn't get out. I remember when the "Central Park 5" story broke in the early 90's, where five little boys were accused of raping, beating, and leaving a young lady in the park for dead. Well eventually, these young men were exonerated, and a movie about their journey came out called "When They See Us". In the movie, there was a scene where one of the exonerated "5" was in prison sweeping, and SWV's "I'm So Into You "video came on the TV monitor. As the song catches his attention, he stops sweeping for a moment, looks at the television and has a personal moment between his current situation and the groove of the song. Mind you, we were well on our way to becoming one of the best-selling groups of our era with our debut album, "It's About Time". Whatever happened in this moment, he started to sweep with so much pride, smiling and bopping his head to our song, but yet, it didn't change the fact that he was in prison.

This is the perfect way to describe how I've felt almost my entire career. I was smiling and singing with two of the most talented women, traveling all over the world, songs in heavy rotation, made a little money, and shared the same stage with some of the industry's best. All of this going on in my life, but yet, I still felt like the prisoner with the broom, but only my broom was a microphone.

The dream wasn't always bad though. It taught me that everyone is not going to believe in you. Everyone will not have your best interest at heart, even if you're paying them. It made me grow up and understand how people worked. Just as fast as you can enjoy something, it can be taken away so much quicker, especially when you are not in control.

As popularity began to grow, my bank account could never catch up with it. It seemed the more I smiled, the more I was challenged and put in some of the toughest situations. It seemed like the dream just didn't want me to be great, and neither did the powers that be in it.

Eventually you take the gloves off and stop fighting, and when this happens, just close your eyes and dream again. You have to remember why you started dreaming in the first place, remember the joy that dreams bring, despite the struggles that may come along with them. The dream I lived may not have been perfect, but it was mine. I was able to do what I love with two amazingly talented women; and I am forever grateful for the many supporters that has sustained us for all of these years, even through our mess, and just trying to figure out what this whole thing was about. Having people that truly believe in you and recognize your gift is a blessing within itself, and I thank God for it all.

# CHAPTER FOUR

## She Touched Me (Part 1)

It was a hot summer day at my parents' apartment on the Grand Concourse in Bronx, NY. This day was special and exciting because it wasn't often, we had company and got to fire up the grill, so we had a lot to look forward to. You know when colored folks get together its always about food and drinks. Anyway, this particular day was really cool because my Uncle Bill and his wife Elsie were coming over. Uncle Bill was always very special to everybody, especially the kids. He was high yellow with beautiful blue eyes to die for.

Thinking of Uncle Bill is always funny because although I was a child, I couldn't help but notice his admiration for womens' breasts lol. Uncle Bill didn't care who you were, married or not, young or old, if you had big beautiful breasts, he was going to be your best friend lol. It made all the sense in the world because his wife Elsie had the biggest boobs I had ever seen. You couldn't help but catch a glimpse of them whenever she was around to be honest. They were very damn distracting for no reason at all.

Speaking of Elsie, she wasn't a beautiful woman at all, but rather very masculine looking with everything on her that says "She's a woman". She kind of remind you of a watered down version of Queen Latifah, very brolic in stature but you can tell she's a lady. I have to mention that Queen is way more attractive than she ever was. Elsie was very friendly with all of my sisters but she was extra friendly with me for some reason. She'd always bring me things like candy and walk me to the store across the street. I never thought anything of it because she was Aunt Elsie, Uncle Bills wife. She was harmless as far as I was concerned, especially since she wasn't a stranger. When I think about our trips to the store, I'd always get this Lollipop that I didn't necessarily want, but I got because she suggested it. The lollipop was good but it was very messy. I had sticky stuff all over my hands and it was tough to get off. I know you're probably wondering what does the lollipop have to do with anything, right? Well, a sticky messy lollipop that was all over my hands, face, and shirt, meant she'd have to take me to the bathroom to get me all cleaned up. I would've never known the events that would take place the next couple of visits-- would change my life and views about love, relationships, and sex for the rest of my life.

**The Bathroom**

I was only 8 years old the first time I was physically touched. Over the course of a three years, I was molested by my Uncles

40

wife Elsie. The one person who was nice to me, would be the one to take advantage of my innocence and take me on a sexual journey mentally that I was way too young to experience. Those trips to the bathroom was nothing more than a ploy for her to be a pedophile. To do to me what she probably did to some other little girl somewhere else. Although it's a little tough for me to talk about sometimes, I can remember this one trip to my mothers' bathroom clear as day. It went like this:

After the trip to the store, Aunt Elsie would lure me into the bathroom so she could wash my hands and clean me all up (yeah right). Now keep in mind, my parents were on the balcony and in no way thought I was in harm's way. Besides, I was still in my own home so there was nothing to really worry about—so they thought.

I remember her turning the water on, which she would leave running to throw everyone off and conceal whatever intentions she had for me. So, Aunt Elsie washed her hands and then she stood me in front of her to wash mines. I can smell the Dial soap that my mother would always get for the bathroom on my hands right now. Not one of my favorite soaps today, but I use it occasionally when I think of my mom.

Hearing the water running made me have to urinate. So, I used the bathroom and as I sat on the toilet I couldn't help but see my aunt in the mirror admiring her huge breasts and big nipples. She groped her breasts and asked, "Do you want some of these"? I replied "yes, I don't have any". She laughed and said

"You will one day, but right now you can have these (referring to her boobs)". I was one excited little kid but didn't know why. I knew nothing at all about what was going on. I guess I had never seen a huge set of breasts so close to me. I didn't know what they were, why they were there, I was just trying to figure out why I didn't have any.

What happened next would change my life forever. My Aunt Elsie had me do the unthinkable to her and she did the unthinkable to me. Looking like a hungry puppy waiting for a meal, she asked me did I want to play with her breasts, and of course-- I said Yes. Very timid and inexperienced, I didn't know what that meant, so she took my small hands and placed them on her each of her breasts focusing mainly around the nipple area. Once I got an understanding of what to do, I asked her, "what is this ball", she laughed and said "that's called a nipple. That's how mothers feed their young kids". It's okay to do that. "That's how little kids get strong", she said. I wanted to be strong. I figure the stronger I got the closer I'd get to having breasts like hers as she promised me.

I was standing up still playing with her nipples which began to get harder and harder. I guess it was starting to feel good to her because she told me to put my mouth on it. I said "How"? She reminded me of the lollipop I had earlier and instructed me to do the same thing to her nipple. I attempted to suck her breasts, but I think I bit it too hard. At this time, she pulled my shirt up and begin to demonstrate on me what I needed to do to her. I will never forget the motion and the warmth of her tongue that caressed my eight-year-old flat chested nipple. I guess that was the moment I began to realize that the nipples immediately communicates with the vagina. It was just different. All I knew was I never had that feeling before. Not that I was supposed to, I'm just saying.

She then groped one of her breasts and put her nipple in my mouth. I did exactly what she asked me to do --I believe I did it right this time because she would grab my head and damn near bury it in her breasts to penetrate it more. As an adult now, it makes my stomach-ache to think that she was having an orgasm from my performance. But that's not all, she took her finger and touched my poopoo. I remember her asking me several times, "does that hurt"? "Does this hurt"? I said no because it really didn't hurt. She didn't stay down there but it was long enough for me to respond to how she touched me. The sound of the refrigerator closing indicated that someone was close by maybe getting a drink or something. My first experience with a child molester had ended abruptly, but not before she told me that this was our secret, not to tell anyone or they would get jealous and we wouldn't be able to do it anymore.

When Uncle Bill and Elsie left to go home that evening, I was so confused. I was haunted by the images I saw in that bathroom. The whole experience was just a little too much for me. I had so many questions and no answers. Was I still a virgin? Did I do something wrong? Why was this such a big secret? I had no answers to my own questions I just played the "quiet" game.

After three years of molesting me, Aunt Elsie would eventually pass away, and all I had was memories. I'd go through middle school confused as hell not knowing if I should be with a boy or a girl. Besides, the only experience I had was with a grown woman who was no longer here to talk to me about my confused mind.

It wasn't until sixth grade, during a sex education class where I first realized what I had experienced wasn't right. I was actually molested. I would sit through class in a sweat trying to get certain thoughts out of my system.

Me being molested by my Uncles wife was my secret until I turned 19 years old. I finally was able to tell my sister Jeanette what happened to me. I never got into depth about this because I was so young, and everyone would feel responsible for what happened to me. I would go on years haunted by the "Elsie" spirit and I displayed it every chance I got.

**Used and Confused**

For a long time, I was so confused about my sexuality or should I say gender wasn't an issue for me. Keep in mind, I was violated before I could even have my first conversation about sex. I never thought about it because I had nothing to compare it too. For a long time, I just didn't understand what was going on with me, how to think, etc. I found myself angry at the woman who did this to me. I needed to talk to her, and she wasn't there for me. She left stuck in my emotions and I found it hard to move on. I hated the fact that I couldn't talk to anyone about our secret. I was left alone trying to find a hiding place. A place to hide this secret in hopes that I'd soon forget. Besides, no one would ever know anyway if I didn't tell them.

But one day, I was lying in my bed over the covers in my parents' full-size bed. The door was open because I had nothing to hide. My father just happened be going to the bathroom and the unthinkable happened. I was caught with my hands in my private parts.my dad walked by and looked in the room before going in the bathroom which was about two feet away. He said, "What the hell you are doing?", I jumped and said, "Nothing". He said, "Don't ever let me see you doing that again you hear?".

Lawd if I could've jumped out the window at that very moment I would've. To hear my father's loud, intimidating voice scared the hell out of me. I knew at that very moment that I must have been doing something wrong. I was a little kid, just trying to touch myself like Aunt Elsie did. It was at this point, I knew what Aunt Elsie did to me was wrong.

# CHAPTER FIVE

## *15 and Pregnant*

"Something isn't right, I'm taking you to the doctor." After getting up in the wee hours of the morning snacking, craving saltine crackers, and ice-cold water, my mother was nobody's fool. This was my routine every night and my mother eventually caught on. She asked, "Why are you up every night eating all the crackers and drinking so much water". I said, "Because I'm hungry Ma". I mean damn, it wasn't like we had a shit load of food in the house anyway, but the fact that crackers and water is not really the normal midnight snack, especially for me, sent Mommy's antennas through the roof. I was young and I would nibble on everything that wasn't good for me like: snickers, cheese puffs, etc. The only time I really ate crackers was with Campbells' Chicken Noodle soup.

"I don't care what you say, something ain't right. I'm taking you to the doctor," my mother said. I looked at her like she was crazy as hell. Thinking to myself, "Why the hell is she tripping, isn't nobody pregnant". I felt confident about going to the doctor because I was still getting my period. There was nothing about little ole me that said "pregnant". No weight gain, breasts didn't grow,no nothing. I had comfort in knowing that I was going to be good money.

The next morning mom called the Harlem Hospital clinic to see if we can make an appointment for a pregnancy test. Luckily, they had a cancellation, so we were able to get an appointment late that afternoon. I don't know what happened to me emotionally between yesterday and today, but I was very uncomfortable. I was suddenly thinking about everything my mother said to me, and my irresponsible behavior in the past.

Me being my usual slow self, I was doing everything I could to take my damn time. Suddenly, shit was hard to find, I lost a shoe, couldn't find my shirt, etc. Mommy couldn't decide what wig to wear and that held us up even more. It was now an hour before we had to be at the clinic, and I guess it's safe to say we were probably running late. On a normal day, our broke asses would save money and take the train, but mom was feeling herself, so we took a taxi.

We finally get to the clinic and head upstairs to the fourth floor. Thirty minutes early, mom decided I should fill out whatever paperwork I had to. Because I was a minor, she had to damn near approve every darn thing. We went to the reception area to sign in and the lady asked, "What time is your appointment ma'am"? I said, "Four o'clock". She asked my mother for her ID so she could verify my appointment and she gave it her.

My mom didn't have a driver's license, so she just showed her a former employment ID. As I began to sign myself in, the receptionist handed my mom a questionnaire for me to fill out on a clipboard, and I did. As I began to read the questions I suddenly I got amnesia. "When was the last time you had sex", "have you ever been pregnant before", "do you have multiple sex partners", etc. I must admit, answering these questions in front of my mother wasn't the most comfortable feeling in the world, especially since she was more focused on the paper than I was. I wonder what my mother was thinking at the time.

As I handed the clipboard back to the receptionist, she proceeded to give me a cup to urinate in. "Put the urine in this cup, write your last name on it, and leave the cup in the window and have a seat," the lady said. Still feeling very confident about me not being pregnant, I sat down and began to read one of the Jet magazines on the table. I wasn't sure how long this was going to take, but it felt like forever! I was halfway through the magazine and I hear my name being called. "Ms. Lyons come back please". I closed my magazine and walked towards the back door, with my mother slowly walking behind me. I honestly think she was more anxious than me.

So, we walked to the back and was escorted to a room. As Mommy and I sat down, the nurse opened the folder, looked at me, and then my mother and said the unthinkable. Of course, it felt like the jeopardy music was playing in my head. What I was about to hear in a couple of seconds felt like it was in slow motion. The nurse looks at me and asks, "What do you want the results to be Miss Lady". I said, "negative" of course. She then looked towards my mother and said, "The test came back positive, you're pregnant". My mother said she's what? "Mrs. Lyons she's pregnant", the nurse said. I was speechless! tears uncontrollably started to run down my face as I quickly looked at my mother face filled with disappointment. "So, what do you want to do", Mom? She said that like it was my mother that was pregnant. That's how things are when you're a minor, out in these streets doing all kind of adult shit that you, yourself can't even fix without an adult. In the saddest face, Mommy looked at me and said, "I can't afford to take care of a baby, you know this". Quickly I interjected and said, "can I get rid of it"?

The nurse informed my mom and I that the hospital had a Planned Parenthood section on another floor. Planned Parenthood back in the day was a women's organization that advocated for women's reproductive health. They offered services from birth control pills, condoms, gynecological services, and early stage pregnancy terminations. It was the place to go for young, poor, irresponsible young girls like me, and they were always packed.

In order for us to proceed, we now had the challenge of seeing how far into the pregnancy I was, which meant I had to take a sonogram. The sonogram gives an image of an ultrasound which doctors use to determine the size of the baby and sometimes the sex of the baby. I couldn't believe all the young people who were in this facility to either get birth control or pregnancy termination, but I had my own shit to worry about now and I was scared to death. Here I am at a clinic, with my mother, trying to see if I can have an abortion at fourteen years old. Luckily, I was able to go straight to the room and get started. I didn't have to get completely naked, Thank God! It was freezing in that place. All I had to do was pull my pants down below my stomach and that's it.

As I lay on the table, the nurse put this sticky kinda gel on my stomach and begin to examine my stomach. Mommy was sitting in the chair following the nurses every stroke trying to figure out what was on the monitor. The noise from whatever it was she was doing was scaring the hell out of me. The more she looked in the monitor, the more she wrote in my folder. she put something in my ear and told me to listen to it. "What is this I'm listening to", I said. "Your baby's heartbeat", she said. She then proceeded to take that instrument out of my ear and sat it on the table. At this point, I'm getting really frustrated and scared at the same time. The nurse looked at me and my mom and said, "Ok, there are two issues". The first one is you won't be terminating this baby, and two, if you were to terminate this pregnancy, we won't be able to do it. "Why, what's going on, I said"? "Well, this baby is due in four months, you're nineteen weeks pregnant young lady". I wanted to literally throw up all the food I ate in the last two weeks and drop dead. My heart was so heavy, and I can imagine what my mom was going through at that very moment. It took everything in me to not look at my mother and her disappointment. It's one thing when you fuck up, but it another thing to fuck up and there's absolutely nothing you can do. As we left, the nurse started to schedule my prenatal appointments with some free prenatal vitamins to start asap.

It was a quiet ride home. In the beginning, we rushed to get to the doctor, but we took the longest way home going back. Where we lived in the Bronx at the time, we had to take two trains and a bus. By the time we got on the bus portion of our ride, everything that transpired that day started to really penetrate my mind. Mom and I sat in different rows on the bus because it was pretty crowded. As I sat down at my window seat staring out the window, I'm not sure what happened to me, but it was at this moment I began to realize whatever I had done to myself, my family, good or bad, it was now my reality and the beginning of my journey. It was then, I pulled my pants under my stomach and began to somehow connect with my unborn child. All of a sudden, I felt free as the mother/child connection began. Every thought that crossed my mind about having an abortion, suddenly went out the window, as I started to connect with my unborn child. I was wondering was this a supernatural thing that happened. Would God give me such a connection even when it was conceived out of sin? This was the part that no one would understand unless they were in my shoes. For these couple of minutes, I didn't give a damn about how anyone else felt about the selfish, immature decision I had made. The reality was, I had a real baby, with a real heartbeat, that was growing everyday inside of me that didn't ask to be here.

# CHAPTER SIX

## *The Next Exit*

After the birth of my daughter Margaret, I really didn't find much time to get out and do all of the fun stuff that teenagers did. Although, motherhood kicked in really quick for me at just fifteen years old, I can't deny the moments that I spent longing to just go in front of the building where most of the kids on my block hung out. But my life had drastically changed. When I made the decision to drop out of high school after getting promoted to the eleventh grade, I immediately started working two part-time jobs because I wasn't old enough to work full time. This took a lot out of me and I was really tired most of the time. Sometimes too tired to be a mother.

From my window on the fifth floor, there were times I'd hear so much excitement going on outside, I often wondered what the hell was going on down there. There were cars driving by with their booming systems—playing music so loud you'd think you were at an SWV concert lol. If I felt like going somewhere with my friends, I never said anything because I knew what the possibilities were—slim to none. Don't get me wrong, I didn't have the kind of mother that just wouldn't watch my baby--in fact—she wasn't even the type that would say no-- I just knew my mother was no longer as young as she used to be and she just didn't have the level of patience (with kids) that she had once before. Once I became a mother, I just never could fix my mouth to ask someone to watch my baby—not even my mother.

This hot summer day I received a call from a gentleman that I met on 125th street in Harlem, NY. I remember him because he had the nicest, loudest car on the block—and of course you can tell he was in the pharmaceutical business, if you know what I mean. He was my kind of guy at the time: handsome, nice wheels, and tax-free money lol. That wasn't the only thing that attracted me to him though. What really sold me was, I had my young baby with me.

I said to myself, if he's attracted to me that's one thing, but if he still finds me attractive walking with a baby that he didn't father—he's probably someone that I should pay some attention to. After all, what the hell did I have to lose. I was a young, attractive, light-skinned, high school dropout with an infant baby that I could barely take care of. I had little where-abouts as to where my daughters' father was, especially after finding out that another girl was pregnant at the same time I was. I guess it's safe to say the day my daughter was conceived, that was the day I literally became a single mother.

It would be a few days before I heard from my little friend again. I was wondering what the hell took him so long to call me. Okay, I know two days doesn't seem like a lot of time, but I guess I was just being a thirst-burger, excited about getting to know my new friend. In fact, he claimed he tried to call me a few times but kept getting a busy signal. He might be telling the truth because in 1988 we didn't have all-inclusive phone plans with call waiting like we have now. All of that was an extra charge at the phone company and my Godmother Jet (whom we were living with at the time) wasn't having that. So if someone was on the phone and another call came in, it would be a busy signal every time. I can't lie, I stayed on that damn phone.

Conversing with my new friend felt like a breath of fresh air. We'd talk for ten minutes here and twenty minutes there. I could tell he was going from block to block checking on his workers and collecting that drug money. There were often times we'd be on the phone and I could hear him arguing with one of his workers because his money was a little bit short. I should've known the way he was talking to the very people that was paying all of his bills that his ass had a bad attitude and very little compassion. But just like a young, dumb teenager who thought she had all the damn answers, I ignored the signs because my new friend had everything going for him—and I wanted to be a part of it.

We made arrangements to go check out a late movie on the following Saturday night which was perfect for me because I'd have enough time to build up the nerve to get a babysitter. I already knew what I was going to wear for my special date: my orange leather and denim hottie shorts, my white long sleeve off the shoulder body shirt with my white lo-top 54.11 reebok sneakers with white ankle socks with the orange ball hanging out. Y'all, I had it all planned out. I had so much on my plate, I could use a break from everything that was and wasn't going on in my life.

Beep, beep!!!! I looked out the window and there he was. This nigga finally shows up after waiting two hours on his ass to pick me up. I was a little frustrated, but still ready to hit the streets and enjoy whatever what was left of my night. Luckily for me, without having to ask, my mother offered to babysit earlier that evening. My daughter was bathed, in clean nighties, smelling like a sweet baby and knocked the fuck out. So, I was good on the home front. Praying that my daughter wouldn't wake up by the time I opened the door, I grabbed my sweater and zoomed my ass down the steps--three steps at a time.

Ole boy was very complimentary, telling me how beautiful I looked and how awesome I smelled. "Damn baby, you smell good as hell", he said. I smiled and replied, "Thank you so much hun". Yep, even back then I was hunning and babeing niggas to death. It was just really sexy and made people feel really special. So, we headed towards the

Tri-borough Bridge on our way to Queens to catch the last movie. It wasn't as easy as looking everything up on a smartphone like we can now. We had to physically go to the location, look in the yellow pages for the number, or if you were lucky enough to have one of those big ass car phones the size of a brick you could always call 411 for information. Nevertheless, we were out of luck. The last movie was sold out, so we decided to grab a bite to eat at a 24-hour diner.

When we finished dinner, it was around 2:30am. It was still hot outside (around 76 degrees), The after-party crowd was just kicking in and the place was getting loud. It was the perfect time to get the hell out of there. So, my date paid the bill and I grabbed my sweater and we were ready to go. After all, since we couldn't see a movie and I was personally full as hell after eating my favorite diner meal: a cheeseburger deluxe, I was ready to go home. We got in the car and sat a few minutes while he looked through his pager. That damn thing was buzzing every other second. All I could think about was who was that trying to contact him. It wasn't a normal beep. You know the difference between someone trying to contact you, you don't answer and that's it. These beeps were more like a wife wanting to know, "where the hell is my husband at this time of night" beeps. I could tell whoever the person was trying to contact him frustrated the hell out of him.

As we left the diner, we headed towards the Brooklyn Queens Expressway (BQE), which was the opposite way from my house. So, quietly I just observed to see how far out we were going, and we were already four miles out. Now, at this point, I'm feeling a little uncomfortable because we never discussed going anywhere other than to see a movie (which never happened) and dinner. On top of that, the frustrating pages that he received all the while we were having dinner. Shit, "maybe he was going to one of his spots to collect some of his drug money", I thought. Which wouldn't have been a problem had we discussed it. I had no idea what was going on.

Taking a chance, but not wanting to add to the frustration, I asked, "Where are we going?". He looked at me and said, "Shorty we going to the crib". I'm like what crib? This is not the direction to my house hun. He said, "Nah shorty we going to my crib to chill for a minute, you know what time it is". Ummm, "No, I don't know what time it is because this wasn't a part of the plan," I said. "I don't understand, are you not taking me home?", I said. I looked over to see his eyes getting real big as I displayed anger and disappointment in my tone. After all, I didn't really know this dude, and the little I thought I knew was through phone conversations—this definitely wasn't the same guy. He totally changed into something that began to make me feel very uncomfortable.

At this moment, I realized I just added to his frustration. He looked at me quickly as he was still driving and said, "Enough with this bullshit, are you fucking or not?". In my head, I was literally going back into time. Thinking of the moment I met this dude and how excited I was about getting to know him. This was about to take a turn for the worse. I took my chance and asked one more time, "Can you please take me home". All hell broke loose.

"Bitch get the fuck out of my car if you aint fucking", he yelled. "Are you serious?", I said. "You heard what the fuck I said. Get the fuck outta my whip, walk home hoe". I felt like someone lit a match and set me on fire. Here I am with a guy that I barely knew, who was obviously very frustrated, and probably didn't feel like taking me all the way back home to the Bronx. I couldn't understand for the life of me how he went from this sweet guy who was very complimentary, to this monster that I never saw coming. All I know is, whomever was paging him one hundred times while we were eating, changed the whole course of the evening. Without going back and forth with this dude, I just opened the car door and got out. I even told the bastard to have a good night. I refuse to let him feel like he had any more power over me. Little did he know, I was crying my eyes out inside.

I couldn't believe this son of a bitch put me out on the Brooklyn Queens Expressway at almost 3:30 am in the morning with hottie shorts on. I had no money at all to get home—not even the $1.15 it costs to take the train home. I believe I had a few quarters to use the pay phone, but I was scared to death to call home. There was no way I could call my mother at this time of morning. She would literally have a heart attack thinking something happened to me—well technically something did happen to me, but at least it wasn't fatal—yet. Right about now, my mother would have fallen asleep sitting in the chair by the window waiting for me to walk in the door. Deep down inside I was hoping this was some sort of a prank or something and he would eventually back his car up and come get me. Boy was I wrong.

Tears were slowly coming down my face as I started to head towards the next exit which was about a half mile down the highway. It was already 76 degrees outside and the pace I was walking took my body temperature up to at least 95 degrees. I was walking so fast I could barely feel my legs moving. The adrenaline just took over me.

I solely relied on my survival skills, street smarts, and Faith in God to keep me alive and get me home safe. Not wanting to draw any more attention to me, I took my sweater and wrapped it around my waist so I wouldn't show so much leg. I wasn't sure what I had to face that night, but I sure didn't want to invite any predators my direction at all. All that trying to be sexy shit went out the window real fast. I wanted to feel like the ugly duckling at that moment.

## The Stranger I Met

There were not many cars on the highway at this time of morning. Approximately three cars would pass me every fifteen minutes. It was a scary ass mess. All I could think about was the dangerous position that I put myself in, and the possibilities of my daughter's mom getting killed, raped, kidnapped, etc. I wanted to get back home to my baby by any means necessary. After about fifteen minutes of walking I finally made it to the next exit. I was scared as hell. From where I was, there were two ways I could go—straight or to the right. I chose to walk towards the right.

At almost 4:00am in the morning, the only thing out in the streets were prostitutes and drug addicts and that's what I ran into. Right under the bridge of the BQE reminded you of the train that ran outside. We call it the L train in New York. It was dark with very few lights and everyone avoided going under there at night. It was the place drug addicts would go to shoot dope, have sex for drugs, and whoever wanted to commit a crime and get away with it—they would. Wasn't anybody saying a damn thing. Most of them were probably too damn high to notice anything even happened. As tears continued to run down my face, I passed a few apartments outside. "Knock, Knock". I waited a few seconds and knocked again. Someone came to the door that sounded like an older Hispanic lady. "What do you want", she said. "I'm stranded can you please help me" (in my crying, lost voice). She said, "I'm sorry, go away before I call the police".

I was sick as hell wondering why she didn't believe that I needed help. After all, I didn't look terrible, and besides the tears that came across my face, I looked well put together. But honestly, who the hell would open their doors for anyone in such a crime infested area? I was convinced that I was just assed out. I knocked on a few more doors and kept walking hoping someone would come out. After finally finding an outside apartment with a little damn light above it, I gave up and sat down. There were three steps that led to the inside of the apartment, and I sat on the middle step as if I was waiting for my mother to come home. I was so mad at myself at this point. I got myself in a mess that I couldn't get myself out of. The good thing was I was still alive, so it didn't get that bad yet besides the rats that I had to run from.

I had no more tears to shed at this point. I was sleepy as hell and thinking about the ass kicking, I was going to get if I finally got myself through this. Lo and behold, I saw an older gentleman walking towards me from across the street. He didn't look like a threat at all, especially after noticing he had on a uniform. I noticed as he got midway, he stopped and looked towards the apartment stoop where I was sitting. It almost looked as if he was trying to see if I was a familiar face—maybe a crazy ass ex-girlfriend, I don't know. As he approached me, I stood up and he asked, "Can I help you, you're sitting in front of my apartment". "This is my stoop", he said. "I apologize sir, but I need some help". "Okay, I'm listening, he said. Shaking my head, embarrassed about my situation, all could say is, "It's a long story". "I'm listening, he said. "I'm stranded after my date put me out of his car on the highway", I said. "I have no money to get home". At this point I'm embarrassed as hell and very annoyed.

He asked, "Is this a joke?" and started to look around as if he was seeing if I was setting him up to get robbed or something. Thinking about this situation once again, my whole body started to cry again. Uncontrollably, tears started to run down my face, "Sir, I am not lying, I'm only sixteen and I have to get home". "Can I just use your phone to call my house"? He said, "Ok, I believe you.

Finally, after almost two hours of knocking on doors and praying that I just come out of this situation alive, I finally felt a level of comfort after running into who seemed to be a good Samaritan. I realized when I got closer to him, the uniform I noticed earlier was that of the United States Post Office. So, now that I knew he worked a government job, I didn't think that I was in any real danger. As he took out his keys to unlock the door, he looked around once again to make sure he was safe before fully opening the door. After all, he didn't know me and I didn't know him.

The both of us had every reason to feel uncertain about each other, but this was one chance I had to take. He then held the door open so I can go in first, and I did. Once we got in, politely he asked, "would you like something to drink? I have water or orange juice". "I'll take a glass of water with no ice please", I said. Although, I really wanted orange juice, I chose water with no ice so I can see through the glass in case he wanted to drop a date rape pill in there or something.

As he went to the kitchen, which was about ten feet away to get the drinks, I unlocked his front door just in case I had to run the hell out of there. I was young for sure, but I wasn't that damn dumb when it came to survival. Especially after the bullshit I just went through, hell no! He was a pretty decent guy it seemed, but I was ready for his ass in case he tried some slick shit. I'm thankful I never had to run out though.

My good Samaritan asked me a few questions before getting his rotary telephone. Of course, you know he gave me the, "you need to be more careful" speech. I got it but damn it was almost five in the damn morning and I just needed to get home. It took everything in me to dial my Godmother's phone number, but I did. "Riiiiiing, Riiiiiing", Riiiiing, Riiiiing,. On the third ring, someone answered—It was my sister Jeanette who sounded like she had just awakened from a deep sleep. "Where's mommy", I asked. "She's sleeping, where the hell are you at this time of morning". I could tell she got up and probably went to the kitchen to wear my ass out—and that she did. When I told her, I needed help and I was stranded because my date put me out of his car, she called me everything but a child of God.

"Why the fuck you go out with some nigga and don't have no money to get home"? "You do some of the dumbest shit", she said. "You not gon kill my mother", she said. All I can do is take this verbal beating because I felt like a complete ass. My sister went on to ask, "How are you getting home, you know we don't have no money"? "I need thirty-three dollars to take a cab", I said. "I'm tired of you worrying mommy. Get home the best way you can". —Click!

My sister hung up the phone on me. I can't tell you how hurt I was, not at my sister, but at myself. The good Samaritan looked at me as if he felt so bad for me. He asked me to call my sister back, he wanted to talk to her. I told him I didn't think It was a good idea because she's really pissed off. "Let's give it a shot", he said. At this point, I dialed the number again and gave him the phone. He asks me my sisters' name, I told him Jeanette. He said "Jeanette, don't worry about it, I'll give her the money to take a cab". I looked at him like he gave me a brand-new heart because I was weak as hell. My sister asked him who he was, and he replied, "Long story, she'll explain it to you when she gets home".

Finally, I was in front of my building and scared to death, I got home about five thirty in the morning, maybe something to six. I lightly knocked on the door and my sister let me in. I ran straight to the bathroom and quickly changed into my pajamas. Just in case my mom woke up, she'd think I was there most of that time. But lo and behold, I was so wrong. I was honest with my mom and explained to her what happened. She was more upset at my judgement when it came to my date. I was looking for the wrong things for all the wrong reasons and it backfired on me. It didn't matter what my punishment was at that time, I was just happy I came out of that shit— and even more happy to be back home with my family and baby. One wrong turn could've gotten me all jammed up and someone else would probably be telling my story today.

Thank God for the good Samaritan who was an angel from heaven to me. He literally saved my life. After calling to tell him that I made it home and thanked him for about thirty minutes, I wouldn't hear from him again until about twenty years later when a stranger hit me up on Myspace to tell me I looked familiar. This story gets better stay tuned.

# Chapter Seven

## PIMP ME

I was sixteen years old and we were about to get evicted for what it seemed like the one hundredth time. We were living on Grant Avenue in the Bronx just barely making it. I remember this apartment so good because all we had were cots in the bedrooms. You know-- the same cot that you borrow/rent-- from the hotel room that folds and rolls. Umm hmm, yep, that was my bed. After losing our furniture and personal belongings at a storage, we were straight up riding it out. We had to literally start all over again. I think "Starting Over" became the soundtrack of my life.

My mother was retired, and I have no idea how she was paying the rent. All I knew was my father wasn't helping with a damn thing. He was busy living his life, sleeping good at night while we struggled. Struggling became normal to me after a while. So much so that whenever we got a break, I thought something was wrong. It was the weirdest thing you know.

I was so sick of packing and moving every other month (it seemed) to a different apartment. I couldn't allow us to get evicted another time. My heart couldn't take it again. I'm sixteen years old with a year-old baby, and all I could think of was Department of Children and Family services getting wind of my homelessness and taking my daughter from me. That was not an option at all. I had to get creative and come up with a plan.

Anyway, as I was thinking and plotting on a way to come up with this rent money, I remembered a rapper/friend of mine whom I will refer to as "Juicy" from Queens that was into some real street shit. I mean he was selling everything from weed, crack, to women. Whatever you needed—he had it! I didn't give a damn, I needed to get this money.

So, long story short, I told "Juicy" my situation and he understood. He would always refer to me as "baby girl". He said, "Baby girl" when do you want to come and meet me so we can talk about your plan? I said whenever is good for me, I just had to make sure my baby was in good hands. So, a few days went by and "Juicy" came to pick me up from the Bronx. It was a real quiet ride in the car because I was nervous as hell. There was something very intimidating about "Juicy".

Although he was very soft spoken, he was very brolic and frightening. As we got on the highway, I already knew whatever this plan was I'd be taking a huge risk. I could possibly go to jail, or even end up dead. I had no idea who he was affiliated with and my insides were trembling like a car that needed a wheel alignment. But the more afraid I was, the more I thought about how beautiful the outcome would be if everything went well. It was time for me to be about that life.

So, we pull up to this house that he owned and all I saw were drug dealers and pretty half ass dressed girls. The house was very intimate with a red light that made it sexy inside. It was not the time to ask any questions, I was still trying to observe the atmosphere and figure out what was going on in there.

"Juicy" introduced me to a girl named "Tee". "Tee" was introduced to me as his "bottom chic". I had no idea what the hell that was, but I was soon to find out. She took me in a bedroom and started talking to me. She was very nice, so I wasn't afraid or felt like I was in any danger. She asked, "Do you know why you're here"? I said, "Yes", I believe "Juice" is going to have me sell or transport some dope, right? "Tee" laughed and said, "No babe, you're here to sell pussy, not drugs". My body went into a state of shock. Suddenly, I felt as if time stopped and I was replaying everything in my head from the moment I saw that eviction notice, to the moment I arrived here. I couldn't turn back now.

It would be a couple of days before I felt like I was ready to get this damn rent money. The bottom chic "Tee" had to take me through training camp for three days. Yes, I had to learn how-to walk-in heels on concrete, what to do in case I was set up by a cop, in case a trick didn't pay up, etc. This was a world that I was very unfamiliar with—well this part. "Juicy" would often remind me of how much pussy I gave up for free, so basically,

I was always a hoe--just a free one. Damn, people can make things sound so terrible sometimes. I felt like a disgusting piece of shit hearing him say this to me that way. In my head, I was cussing his big ass out, but in real life, the truth may set you free.

28th Street and 11th Avenue in New York City, was an area saturated with everything that God warned us about. It was literally Sodom and Gomorrah. Pimps, hoes, drug dealers, drug addicts, homeless people, beggars, and most of all- clients. I can't lie, it looked like a complete circus. It was the moment of truth and my turn to literally put my money where my mouth is. "Tee" was still the boss lady, and I was told to follow her lead at all times. If she moved, I moved—that was the plan.

## A Change of Heart

As "Tee" and I walked on the strip, a white Ford Explorer SUV pulled up on the side of the street. "Tee" said "Get in the back seat", and I did. As we pulled off I could hear her ask the client, "So what do you want". He answered, "a blow job". I'm sure we all know what a "blow job" is right? but for those conservatives living under a rock—it's basically a penis in your mouth.

"Tee" asked the client how would he like it, with/without a condom? At this point, I'm scared to death, shaking like hell and disgusted at what was about to take place. I'm thinking about the foot that would be in my ass had my mother and family knew what I was up to trying to save the family from getting evicted, but I refused to get put out with my daughter.

How much is it without a condom, the Client asked? $60 with a condom and $100 without, said "Tee". Of course, he wanted to feel the fullness and the warmth of the whole experience. so "Tee" went with it. For those of you who are familiar with this area of New York City, you'd know that anywhere past 9th Avenue is dark as hell. So, we drove around the corner and parked. As the Client unzipped his pants to expose himself, "Tee" put a liquid on her hands. I'm not sure what kind of liquid it was, but maybe it was emotion lotion or KY jelly, she then bent over and went towards his penis and proceeded to give him head. All I could hear was the sound of her pleasuring him like a pro. She was so good it was all over by the time I counted to 20. The Client ejaculated in her mouth and it was a done deal. "Tee" opened the car door, spit it out and told me to collect the money-- which I did. We got out the Clients vehicle, went to "Daddy's" car (which she called him, but I called him "Juicy") to give him what we just collected and freshen up. "Tee" rinsed her mouth out with Listerine that was so strong it smelled like it could wake up the dead. She went to a nearby fire hydrant that was on--normal in NYC-- and washed her face and poopoo. At this point, I'm so disgusted at what I just saw I just wanted to go home. I never wanted to see a penis or "Tee" again.

As crazy as it seems, what appeared to be "the perfect plan", was ruined in a matter of minutes. I've come to the realization that this was not me at all, and I didn't give a damn if we had to go to a homeless shelter if my family and I were together. I told "Juicy" I had something to tell him. He said, "What's wrong "baby girl"?" I started to cry and told him, "This isn't for me", and "I couldn't do this".

There was a long pause. I could feel him looking at me as I held my head down looking like a lost, slutty puppy. As I picked my head up, I could hear him say, "Baby girl, I'll let you fly". I said, "For real?". He said, "Yes, I don't want you to do anything you don't want to do". I told him there was something out here that was much bigger than this. I wanted to be an entertainer, but definitely not this kind.

I didn't know what to do. Should I thank him for the opportunity? Lol. I just wanted to put my real clothes on and get the hell out of there—which I did. I couldn't leave out of there fast enough. "Juicy" and I hugged each other as if he was just dropping me off at the airport. I couldn't believe my so called "Pimp" just hugged me and let me go.

After this experience, I never looked at a penis the same way. It would take a long time before I would be able to attempt to perform oral sex on a man and I'm still not one hundred percent there. Every time I think of it, I see images of that man's white penis going into Tees mouth. It's a real struggle for me.

# Chapter Eight

## *Stranger on MySpace*

Social media is not my favorite thing in the world, but somehow, it has a way of connecting us to things and people that we usually wouldn't be able to reach any other way. But in today's world, we must engage, or we will be left behind. One of my favorite things to do on the internet is looking for new music and explore the massive amounts of "new talent" in the world.

One day, I just happen to be on a site called Myspace, a music sharing site where professional and aspiring singers and musicians share their music with listeners. It allows singers and musicians to expose their music to many listeners at one time. I just happened to be on the site and saw that I had a message. Being that fans usually follow seasoned and established musicians and singers, many direct messages me and try to sell me on their gift, or just to say hello in exchange for some good advice. I just so happened to have a little time on my hands, and I read a message sent to me.

"I know this may be a little strange, but I believe I know you. You look very familiar to me," the person said. I quickly clicked the person profile, but that didn't help either. In fact, it was a picture of some art, and the other one was a quote. I really was lost at this moment and had no clue. The only information that was clear to me was that whoever this was, it was a man. "Where do you think you know me from? Did we go to school together?" I asked. He laughed and said, "I don't think so, I'm much older than you, about 11 years older, I believe".

Now, I'm really lost because if he's that much older than me, I'm thinking he's mistaking me for one of my sisters. "So, keep going," I said. He said, "I told my wife that you looked like a young lady that I helped get home years ago. I'm sorry if it's not you, I don't want to put her business out there." I immediately told him to call me. I gave him my cell phone number, and he called immediately. I'm not sure what lead me to give this man my phone number, but this had to be God. I don't even like to hear the phone ring half the time. There was something in his communication with me that made me want to listen to his story, especially since he wasn't trying to sell me any music or anything. Something in my spirit told me that this was for real.

He called me, and my nerves suddenly were all over the place. There was something about this man's voice that was very familiar to me, but I just couldn't put my hand on it. "You look like a young lady that I helped years ago," he said.

"Help do what?" I said. "Years ago, I helped a young girl

get home who was stranded, I believe after a date had gone wrong." "AHHHHHHHHHHHHHH!!!!!!!!!!!". I screamed and dropped the damn phone. My whole body started shaking, and I started to cry so bad. You are fucking kidding me, I cried. "Were you that girl?" he said. "Yes, that was me," I said, screaming and sniffling all over the damn phone. "How did you know I was the same person after all these years have passed?" I asked. He said, "It was the ponytail that I remember because that's how you had your hair that night."

I told him there wasn't a day that went by that I didn't think about how nice he was to me. I believe he literally saved my life. I really don't know what would've happened to me had he not helped me out. I told him to give me his address so I can send him something, and he did. I sent him a "Thank You" package with some fun stuff in there. In the bag were an SWV CD, a t-shirt, and a card with $1000.00 in it. At the time I couldn't afford to pay him back the $33.00 that it took for me to get home in a cab to the Bronx from Brooklyn, but I had enough money now to pay it forward, and I did.

A few weeks passed, and now, my phone rang. It was the stranger on myspace. He called me in tears now thanking me for the "Thank You" package I sent him weeks earlier. "OMG," you don't know what this means to me." "This is nothing but God! he said. I'm thinking, damn he sounds like me when I first spoke to him on the phone. "This gift came right on time." As we continued to talk, he was able to calm himself down. He informed me that he was in the middle of a child support case. He went through a nasty divorce, which caused him a slight financial setback. This would eventually have an effect on his child support payments. He's never been late, but his ex was doing everything in her power to destroy him because he moved on. Apparently, the money I sent him came a day before he was due in court. He was a month behind on his payment and owed the court $700. It was a blessing in disguise. Had he not come up with that money, he would've been locked up for thirty days.

All I could do is say "Thank You Lord" for blessing me so that I can be a blessing to others. Just to know this made me so happy inside. I believe this is part of the reason why God has kept me covered after all these years.

# CHAPTER NINE

## *My Mother's Heart*

My mom was born May 14, 1928 somewhere in Atlanta, Ga. I say that because we have no record of my mom being born in a hospital, a home or anything. Shit, I don't even think she had a real birth certificate. My mom was an original Georgia Peach (my dad from Macon, Ga.), so I guess it's safe to say that I'm part Peach and part Apple—I'm cool with that. I wasn't just another New Yorker who moved to Atlanta because the cost of living was cheaper. I really had roots down there—those good ole southern roots.

Mommy was one of the finest women you could ever want to meet. She was short, thick thighs, and would walk in some heels like it was New York Fashion Week—confident and so matter of factly. She was going to get the attention in the room, not even asking for it. Now, I can truly understand where I get my hospitable personality from. I can honestly find comfort in saying that for a long time I gave way more than I received. If I had, you had, and if I didn't have to give, I'd try and find it.

That was my mom all day.

My mother would take someone in our home quick. If you said your mom was abusing you, your husband left you and you were homeless, or maybe you were just too intoxicated to drive home, chances are—you were going to spend the night at our house. When it comes to spending the night over at our house, one person comes to mind. My mother had a friend named Theresa that she'd hang out with from time to time. Theresa had bad gum disease, which caused her to lose some of her teeth. You know it's always the one with the worst teeth that do the most talking. Well, maybe she couldn't afford dental care, shit—neither could we. Nevertheless, she was still a sweet person.

Anyway, this one Saturday night Theresa and mom were hanging out at the local community bar on 161st Street and Gerard Avenue. Right across the street from Yankee Station. This particular night, Theresa was binging on alcohol, so mom allowed her to take a cab with her to spend the night at our house. Chile, this woman was so intoxicated that any man looking to get in some trouble with a woman that night— Theresa would've been the perfect target. She couldn't even tell you her last name. She was staggering and falling against the wall. It was a mess.

It was about 2am when I heard mom and Theresa come in the house. I was at the house by myself this night, pregnant and cranky as hell. It was so peaceful and quiet, but we had these old wood floors that were loud as hell. No one could ever sneak in that apartment. We didn't have real bedroom sets, so I had to sleep on a cot. Yes, the same cot that you borrow from the hotels that rolls and folds. Hey, at least I had somewhere to sleep, don't judge me.

As Theresa makes her way into my room, she plopped down on the bed so hard almost making the cot fold. If you can imagine half a body on the bed, and the other half on the floor with her legs wide open as wide as an opened umbrella—That's how she fell asleep that night.

I was happy that Theresa was safe, but once this woman found her rhythm, she snored like a cow. As a teenager, I couldn't stand sleeping with anyone who snored this loud. I'm pregnant, tossing and turning, trying to get comfortable again after being awaken by our hard, loud ass old wooden floors— and now my mother's pissy drunk friend, who was annoying the hell out of me.

From a scale of one to ten, with ten being the highest, Theresa was definitely a damn eleven. She was so loud I'd throw shoes at her to shut her up. She'd wake up a little after feeling that sting on her leg, but by the time you count to three, it was back to snoring like a cow again. After throwing a few different shoes at my mom's friend, I'd come to the realization that this was going to be my reality. Either go to sleep through the snoring or sit up and be mad. I huddled myself in those covers and soon after I was knocked out cold. Theresa woke up the next morning asking, "Where all these shoes come from?". My mom would've killed me had she knew what I did, but it sure is funny now.

Mom just had a heart for people. If she had, you had. She was the kind of person that could never say no. That trait ended up being a blessing and a curse. She'd often help people that eventually took advantage of her kindness, but mommy would never change who she was for anybody. She was the type of person that would find good in the evilest person, which explains how she was able to tolerate my abusive father for so long. Everyone loved and respected her. I used to love to hear the kids acknowledge my mother, "Hey Miss Margaret". She'd reply, "Hey baby how you doin". She would always greet everyone with a smile, even if her front tooth came out that day and she didn't have time to glue it back in, at that moment it didn't matter.

Mommy also was a stickler when it came to certain things. If you wanted to piss my mother off, let her see a boy's pants sagging, or hear the sound of snot in your nose while she's trying to eat her food. She despised hearing someone blowing their nose in any setting, even if it was your own home. Mommy would remove herself immediately from that setting. I know for sure if my mom was alive and well, she'd be very disappointed in my son, and the way these young'uns wear their pants damn near to their knees. She would repeatedly tell them to "pull your pants up young man".

For some reason, she could still see the good in anyone who did wrong. And I believe she got her first piece of training from my father who was the ultimate jerk.

## Loving an Abuser to Death

I was in third grade when I first saw first-hand what domestic abuse looked like. After school one day, I ran up the steps like a flying saucer in space, and I don't know why. Most of the buildings in the Bronx didn't have any elevators, so we had to walk and run everywhere we went. When you have to use the bathroom, it's the worst thing ever. In my case, I had to run up four flights of stairs. I was young, on the track team, so that was lightweight to me.

Just like a kid, I always looked forward to my mother's greeting when I came home from school, "Hey baby, how was your day?". As I walked towards where she was, I noticed she was facing the window and never looked at me. Not mommy at all, she'd always stick her head out and acknowledge her youngest child. I also noticed the sound of her voice was very different. Typically, my mother's voice was high (when excited), and clear when she spoke, unless perhaps that annoying tooth in the front of her mouth fell out—which it would do from time to time. Mommy would get some crazy glue and glue it back together. This time it sounded more like a slurring type of sound. Maybe like a person who just had a slight stroke. Whatever the case, it wasn't my mother's norm.

As I went closer to her, it was apparent why my mother kept looking out the window. She was hiding her face, trying to conceal the beating my dad had just put on her a few hours earlier. I believe this was the first time I realized I was a cusser. As I tried to console my mom and ask her who did this to her, she wouldn't say anything, but "I'm okay baby." In the meantime, I hear my father come out of my Godmother's bedroom trying to sneak out the front door. He was trying to leave before I got home from school, but I caught his ass. I grabbed what looked like a vacuum cleaner and headed straight to the door.

"You motherfucker, why you hit my mother?". My mother's lip was so big, and her mouth was so swollen it looked like she had a nasty, bloody allergic reaction. She was almost unrecognizable. The size of her lip affected her ability to speak clearly, which is what caused the slight slur in her words as she spoke to me. I was just a little girl, who didn't give a damn about this being my father.

This man was a monster to me. My mother was such a short woman, 5'1 to my dad's 6'2, absolutely no threat to him at all, so I couldn't understand why he did this. All I can remember was me grabbing the vacuum cleaner, running out the door, aiming that vacuum cleaner straight at my fathers head. I'm angry as hell at this point. I didn't care about the ass whooping that may have awaited me. I was an eight-year-old kid, protecting my mother from a man who was supposed to love and care for her. The sad part was, he couldn't blame it on the alcohol because there was no alcohol. Unfortunately, was who my father was—a coward with a big mouth. From that point on, I was no longer daddy's girl.

That wouldn't be the last beating my mom took from my dad, and I'm sure it wasn't the first. What the hell was wrong with him? My sisters and I would begin to see patterns of this behavior, and just like a battered woman—my mother always protected him. No matter what the abuse, physical or verbal, whenever we would fix our lips to say something or mentioned anything about his abuse, her only words to us would be, "He's still your father." My sisters and I got so used to hearing this, but what the hell did this mean? We knew he was our father, but was she trying to say in so many words that the relationship we had with him as his children were different than the relationship, he had with her? The whole "he's a good father, but a terrible husband," we'd never understand.

Mommy always made sure that her kids were okay, and every other kid for that matter. She didn't have much, but she gave us everything she had, especially when my father left. I guess there was no choice there. After he left her stuck with all these damn bills she couldn't afford, it just got rough for all of us. There were times we would have to boil water on the stove to bathe because we couldn't afford to pay the water bill. We never complained. Having lights on in our house was a luxury for us. It seemed like we would get our lights cut off every time the bill was paid. Whenever my mom would pay the bill, which was never the whole bill, we would have just enough light for about a week, and then we were back to lighting candles. Mommy never complained about anything, even if it was terrible.

I have to give it up to my older sister Maleia, who sacrificed so much of her youth, helping my mother out with bills. Only a teenager, my sister Maleia tried to help my mother out a lot financially, even putting her job on the line, but we just couldn't make it work. She dropped out of college (something she regrets today) to work full time to help mommy out with the bills. Employed as a bookkeeper at Food Emporium supermarket in Manhattan at just seventeen years old, she had access to a lot of money. Thinking she could replace the money before the drawer was counted, my sister Maleia stole a few hundred dollars out of the til to help Mommy out with the bills. The sad part was they found out what she'd done; the good part was she was such a good worker they just made her pay the money back because she was honest about it. She ended up keeping her job. Jeanette and I really couldn't do much but get along with each other at this point lol. All of this and we still didn't complain. This was our "normal."

Being a housekeeper, mommy only made a little over eight dollars an hour, and we all know how far that could go. Now and then, hotel guests would leave her tips, which were always a blessing, but it never made up for what my father wasn't giving. My mother would use some of her tip money to treat us to Chinese Food. Yes, a five-dollar meal at one time was a treat for my sisters and me, and we enjoyed every minute of it.

I can imagine how my mother felt. She'd work extra hours to try to make sure her kids just had a roof over their heads, but nothing she ever did would shake. Mommy would borrow money from here and there, this person and that person, not knowing she'd be getting herself more buried in a whole. I knew things were going too far when two white men knocked on our door, asking to speak to her. That's when you know shit is real when the white man in a suit comes knocking on a door in the hood. He happened to be some loan shark.

After several embarrassing evictions, the responsibility was just too much to bear. Bouncing from apartment to apartment, and eventually being escorted out by the NYC Marshals, I guess we were officially homeless. We put our belongings in storage, and after a few months, we'd get evicted out of there too. We lost a lot of items that held a lot of sentimental value, especially family photos, when we were kids. We would then go to live with my Godmother Jet on Anderson Avenue, in the Bronx. Jet had a one-bedroom apartment in the building we used to live in. Her doors were always open. But, with three other bodies, it was a full house. Thank God she had a let-out couch and a high-riser daybed. We ended up making it work, but it wasn't the most comfortable situation. We were just happy to have a place to stay.

Mommy would soon retire from her housekeeping job, leave for Atlanta to be with her family, and never looked back. Atlanta became her home once again, and it seemed like she was the happiest there. For some reason, this short, thick, fast-paced woman would eventually slow down once she got around the people who she felt loved her. After suffering a couple of strokes, my mother's health started to deteriorate.

All these years she was fighting for a life in New York that the city didn't offer her. If my father wasn't beating her up, this thing called life was—that was until she transitioned in Piedmont Hospital a day before my sister Jeanette's birthday, January 23, 1995. What a way to celebrate. I believe my mother died of a broken heart. Life just had a way of beating her down to the point where she just got tired of fighting and gave up.

I always tell people, as sweet as my mother was, her quality of life should have been better than it was. Not awful in the sense that she was just never happy because it was the small things that my mother appreciated. But, the mother I knew was a dreamer. She wanted more for herself and her kids, but somehow, couldn't find her way out the rut. No matter what happened to us, mommy went out of her way to make sure we didn't find out—but somehow, we did. She did earn a nursing certificate throughout the years, but I have no idea why she didn't pursue it. I guess now it didn't matter anymore.

On her dying bed, my mother told my father, "Lawrence, you will never meet another, Margaret." Oh, boy was she right. After my mother's funeral, we found out that my mother and father were never married, only common law marriage, which was legal at that time. That wasn't good enough for me. My feelings towards my father started to change at that moment.

But I will say this, my mother took her last breath loving her some Larry Lyons.

# CHAPTER TEN

## *He's Still Your Father*

### (An Open Letter to my deceased father)

Hey daddy, how are you? I would have called you on the phone, but you always complained that your phone bill always went from $12.00 to $33.00 whenever we'd come to visit you lol. I figured this way was a little better anyway because you have nothing but time, right? Before I wrote this letter to you, I had several conversations with both sides of the family. I'm sure you wouldn't be surprised at what they had to say about you. Nevertheless, I had my own experience with you.

I promise I won't keep you long, I just have a few things that I'd like to get off my chest. As I write this letter, I'm feeling very emotional, for many reasons of course. One is because you were the first man I've ever loved, and the first man to ever break my young heart. I used to be such a daddy's girl, looking forward to you coming home after work so I could run and get some coins out of the change-bag you brought home after driving the yellow cab that you owned. Not many people owned their cab in NYC, so I was very proud of you. I got some good candy with that change daddy. I always wondered, did you ever notice any of that change missing? lol. Oh, and thank you so much for the family fun days at Rye Play-land. We had so much fun there. It was those times that made me the happiest about our family, because we were able to take our minds from what was really going on in our home. As a young girl, I was always afraid of you and I'm sure the rest of my sisters were too. You were loud and very obnoxious at times, and that's when you were sober. Do you remember when Maleia was young and you made her eat cabbage out the garbage because she was finished eating? Or the time you kicked Jeanette in her back as she walked down the hill in front of her friends? Why would you do something like that? Do you have any idea what that did for their self-esteem? Or you just didn't care at all. After all, you wouldn't have been yourself if you weren't breaking someone down huh?

What happened when you were younger that made you so angry? Were you ever abused in any kind of way? I was told back in the day when you guys were living in Macon, Ga. Big Mama had one potato to cook for the whole family. You got angry and threw the potato in the woods so no one could eat. Why would you make everyone suffer and starve because you were angry? I'm sure it was probably something dumb. I guess that was the beginning of what I consider to be a monster being born —and a monster you were.

Let's Talk about my mother for a minute. Do you remember her? Yes, Margaret Lyons, the one that you hated enough to punch her in the face when you were drunk and angry. The one you never loved enough to officially make her your wife and give her the wedding you gave the other woman who would eventually take you down. Yeah daddy, we found out the truth. No ceremony, no ring, no nothing!! Only common law marriage. You Just dragged her until she took her last breath. Agreeing to a surgery that you knew her heart was too weak to take. It all makes sense now.

You were dating my mother's neighbor at this time, remember? Yeah, the one you'd eventually marry and make an honest woman of and the one you said would eventually kill you. Well, I guess you know how that story went don't ya? Do you know, the day of your funeral, it was one of the worst days of my life? Not because you passed away, but because your wife—who you'll run into up there by the way—separated your children in the car arrangements. She purposely put your love children in the lead car and my mother's kids about three cars behind. Your funeral was the worst Daddy. You looked so terrible they had to take you out of the chapel to fix your face several times. You definitely weren't ready to be viewed, but we had no say at all.

Oh, and did you know that your children never even made the program? No poem, no song, no nothing! I personally felt like a stranger at my own father's funeral. Everyone who got up to speak knew the Larry they just met, not the Larry everyone else knew for 10, 30, 40 plus years. It's bad enough most of my memories of you in life were bad, but in death it sucked even more. Why didn't you put anything in writing Daddy? You always said if you passed away there would be a letter addressed, "To my girls", but we never received it. Til this day, we always wonder what was in that letter, or if there ever was a letter at all. I was hoping maybe it was an apology to my mother. Or even an apology to your only girls.

Daddy, I just want you to tell me why you left me and my sisters. I was only ten years old. If it was my mother, you beat her so much she probably would've dealt with you stilll cheating and living a double life, as long as you were there with us and being a father to your girls. But even that was too much work for you. Was being a father that complicated? Was that level of responsibility way too much to handle? We barely saw you, and you were only at the YMCA in Harlem. You never paid child support for any of us; leaving Jeanette and Maleia to scrape up money from boyfriends and working their tails off trying to help Mommy. They were only teenagers, and poor Maleia gave up being a teenager because she had to help pay rent. Jeanette would even help Mommy with her summer youth jobs. You moved us from a modest apartment on Anderson Avenue, to a nice high-rise on the Grand Concourse. Oh yeah, this was a nice, expensive apartment, but once we got settled you bailed out on us, knowing damn well my mother couldn't afford that rent alone. We came home several times to find that the Marshals put the locks on the door starting the eviction process. While you were loving on women and sleeping well every night, we were getting put out of our apartment you set us up in and left us uncovered. Mommy tried her best, but she couldn't bounce back for some reason. Couldn't you have paid half the rent and we figure the rest out? Damn Daddy that's fucked up!

Well, men like you have screwed my life up. I wanted my father's hugs, but some strange guys hugged me instead. Daddy, I've been getting hugs from strangers ever since you abandoned us. I've been physically and verbally abused by strangers I thought were boyfriends. I thought they were there for me, but they used me just like you used women—for sex and personal gain. A few of them were very intimidating just like you and he would eventually kick my ass when I was only fourteen years old—just like you did my mother—and I still loved him. It scared the hell out of me because I saw myself getting weak like my mother was for you, but unlike her, I walked away from his ass.

I never understood why my mother never stuck a knife through your chest. That's what I said I'd do if a man even looked like he wanted to hit me. I almost came close Daddy. This dude I was dating yelled at me and got in my face and I was ready to take him out. I had the knife right under my pillow. But just like you, it was the brown liquid that sent him to that dark place, and he thought he was taking me with him—NOT! The next day he didn't remember anything that happened. That relationship was over. I don't drink alcohol to this day because of the fuckery that went on when I was little, but it seems to be my son's closest friend. He has a lot of your ways and I'll leave it at that. I think I probably got pregnant by someone with a Larry spirit.

Well, I can say that I applaud you for giving my little sister Tay Tay a good father/daughter experience. She loves you to death and always have. The father that she remembers, that's the father we always wanted, but never got. If we could've gotten even thirty percent of what you gave her, we would've been satisfied. But, it's okay now daddy, it's over now. I had to get this off my chest because I'm no longer afraid of you. I've carried this burden for years and I hated you for a long time. I was a daddy's girl one minute and then something went wrong. Not only did I hate you for how you did my mother, but how you made us suffer for it as well. Nevertheless, I think you've gotten your share of beatings daddy. You died miserably. You married a woman who never loved you like my mother did and she slowly contributed to your demise. We heard from her family that she was into voodoo, hmmm. You were bed ridden with bed sores and all. Not like you at all. I'm going to end this letter by saying "I Forgive You Daddy", and I know Mommy forgives you too. She always did.

I guess I'll leave you with one of your favorite sayings, "You gotta be tough kid, you just gotta be tough". I have been tough ever since. You can finally Rest in Peace sir. And last but not least, my mother would want me say, "You're still my father".

Love Always your baby girl LeAnne😔😔

# CHAPTER ELEVEN

## She Touched Me (Part 2)

Ilearned in my first year of middle school that what happened to me was not only wrong, but against the law. I could finally put a name to the act—Child Sexual Abuse and/or Pedophilia:

After getting acquainted with some of the kids in my school I realize I wasn't the only one that was sexually abused. There were many kids in my school who were removed from their homes because of the same thing. The only difference was the kids were violated by their fathers, uncles and some by their mothers' boyfriends—but not their aunt. It was a terrible thing. You'd never believe the level of dysfunction going on in these young peoples' homes. Many would go unnoticed or swept under the rug, just like all the other mess that's kept quiet in our community.

There was a lot of grown up talk amongst the kids there. I couldn't believe how experienced those kids were. They were wearing sexy clothes, high heeled shoes and had a mouth on them that will suspend them for the whole school year. Not to mention, most of the girls there were very well developed to be so young. Of course, I felt out of place with my underdeveloped ass lol. By the way, I'm still looking for my boobies though Come on Jesus what you are waiting on sir? lol

Half the school were already sexually active, and believe it or not, some of them was having same sex relationships too. What the hell was I walking into? Here I am, twelve years old, not knowing how to process everything that fell in my lap the last few years and now this. All this shit wide open all in my face. It wasn't until I met a few of the kids at school that I learned what a lot of this stuff was. it was normal for the kids to gossip about everything they knew about the other kids' lives, and sometimes they even knew some of the school faculties business. Every time someone walked by it became, "Look at Linda, she still wets the bed", "Look at the two sisters, they gave me and my boy head in the stairway", or "Look at Jeffrey, his mother is a hoe". But then one of the kids came to PTA with their mom and the students were like, "Look at Keisha's mom, she likes pussy", and they would laugh. Umm Okay, in the back of my head I had no idea what the hell any of that meant.

I was at the age now where boys started to like me, and I started to give them some attention as well. Every now and then the images of my molestation years earlier would come to my head and I had absolutely no control over it at all. Because the very person that I shared this secret with was now dead and gone, I figure if I just try my best to like boys the way they liked me, everything will be okay. But that feeling is similar to putting a Band-Aid on a wound when you actually need to have surgery. I figure the only way to figure out who and what I was, was to put whatever I was feeling into action. I didn't know how feel sometimes. I just knew I felt more comfortable in a certain space. I knew deep in my heart I loved everything about a boy—his smell, his walk, etc. But for a long time, I had to figure out how to enjoy men sexually without feeling like I was being raped or used. Sex was always so damn rough and pointless. I didn't realize until after it was over how much of the whole experience was for him, and not me.

I had the hardest time trying to figure out what and who I was. I didn't know if I was the L, G, B, T, or Q. I just always felt admiration for pretty women and handsome ass men, but not in a sexual way. It didn't matter the gender, if there was a connection, that's just what it was. I believe the strangest part of it all was it had very little to do with the physical. I could be with a guy and not sleep with them, and the same with a girl. It wasn't the sex at all, even though I preferred kissing a woman over a penis digging in my back any day. For me, it was the gentleness and the warmth of a body. The tone in which the way she spoke and the friendship. Regardless of what, if there was no connection, it didn't matter one way or another. I had no control over my feelings and who I chose to love. It was the strangest thing I ever had to experience in my life-- and I had to do this alone. I didn't want my family to know anything about what I was feeling or engaged in. I was craving all the things I experienced as a young girl and I wasn't going to slow down until I got my fix. I had to find out some things for myself, but I had to keep this a secret.

As I got older, I couldn't believe the many women that were attracted to me. It was so exciting that I had this secret and it almost became like a game that I played to make me believe it wasn't real. I can honestly say, I totally understand why some people who struggle with identity don't come out quickly or come out at all. It's really a personal thing especially when it's a tug of war with both sexes. It's confusing as hell. Even though I didn't know how to identify myself, my secret and being sneaky was exposed when I was around twenty something years old on the road.

## I Kissed a girl and I liked it

The first time I really kissed a girl it was the best shit ever! It felt so much different than kissing a boy. It was so different that if I closed my eyes and someone was to kiss my lips, I'd know immediately if it was a girl or a boy. I can't explain it other than this kiss was the best kiss since "Mr. Tongue". both of those tongues felt like they belonged together. That kiss was so sexy and good, I was willing to risk it all—literally lol.

We were on tour at the time with some of the other artists when we were managed by Flavor Unit. At this time, I was dating a gorgeous young lady who was a few years younger than me. We were probably together around six months at this time. No one knew anything, especially not my family. She was around, but no one really knew the extent of our friendship. Anyway, to keep my secret, I would always have her fly in the night before we were scheduled to arrive at the hotel. I would call the hotel and add her name to the room. This would allow her to get a key, so she'd be there in the room when I got there and risk the chance of bumping into anyone. Yeah well, that lasted for a few weeks until this one damn day everything I didn't want to happen happened.

On a normal day, we'd check in, and the bellman would load our bags on the cart to be taken upstairs. Once he got up there, he'd take my bags and sit them by the door and leave. But not this day. I have no idea how my road manager at the time ended up being the bellman this day, but she ruined my secret. Instead of her doing what the bellman usually does which is sit the bags by the door, she decides to take the bags all the way in the room, meeting face to face with my friend. The next time I saw her, her sarcastic ass would say, "Lelee, there's a girl in your room" lol. My heart fell out of my body and to the floor. When I got in the room all we could do was laugh at each other. That was pretty much how it all happened. From that moment, that's when all the curiosity, and questions would start.

After that experience, I think everyone looked at me different. Not necessarily in a bad way, but in a way that whenever we would connect eyes it would be funny as hell. One of those, damn how long has this been going on? and Why you didn't say anything before? Lol. UUUGhhh, maybe because there was really nothing to tell. I did things the way I did it because it wasn't something that I wanted people to know. No offense, but I wasn't sure I understood myself at that time. or what was going on with me. There were times I would be in a relationship and would be in tears. The tears would lead to hurt, the hurt would lead to violence. Nothing never worked, and things started to get really emotional and dysfunctional. I didn't want to be there at all. I prayed that God would bring me back to what I felt like at five years old before anything happened to me. I didn't want to be a part of any of it anymore. It was too painful to bare.  There was a time I didn't like studs because they looked like the woman that molested me. It took me a long time to get over that, but I did.

## There are never any real secrets

I used to hear a lot of things about me throughout the years about me being gay. Did it bother me? Not as much as it bothered me when my family had to deal with it. When I was out there being young and all over the place, I was having a ball. I experienced everything I wanted to, and I'm cool with my decision because it gave birth to a lion. I learned a long time ago-- while everybody is all up in your business, they don't have a heaven or hell to put you in.

I've learned to accept the fact that I was violated by an adult, but when I got older, I kissed a girl and I liked it. As long someone else is involved in your mess, trust me, someone else already knows. I got to a point in my life where I got sick of people remote controlling me. As long as what I was doing wasn't hurting anyone, why did anyone care? The only way to not be exposed, don't do it! We are so consumed in other people shit that we can't focus on our own lives.

There is a lesson in everything that we do, whatever you get out of that experience make it count for your Life!! There's been way too much airtime spent on worrying about who this person sleeping with, and who that person sleeping with. I've been guilty of that too. When I meet a guy, I'm quick to ask all my gay friends have they ever had an encounter with him. I love the gay boys to pieces, but I'm not interested in dating a man who likes penis—top or bottom, I'm not interested and that's my choice.

Be who you are, and don't worry about what society thinks. We all have to exist in this one world, and when its over, its over. Being nosy and bullying someone because of a sexual preference is not cool and definitely not worth someone taking their own life. Let Love Win Always!!

# Chapter Twelve

## *My First Apartment*

I lived at The Renaissance hotel in Times Square for about three months until I found a permanent place. I was finally out of my Godmother's apartment in the Bronx, but technically I was still homeless. Now don't get me wrong, I was forever grateful for my current situation, but I was an adult now who finally wanted to experience what everyone meant when they said, "There's no place like home". My group had just finished a tour and I felt like I was ready to take the leap. So, I hired celebrity Realtor Susan Perry, to find me the perfect place. You can't imagine how excited I was. Finally, after sharing a bed with my sister for so many years, to barely having a bed at all with all the evictions—I was finally about to get my own shit.

Although I was in New Yorker at heart, I knew for a long time I wanted to have my first place in New Jersey. I'd always take frequent trips with my Godmother Jet and her friend Mrs. Brenda to ShopRite. ShopRite was a huge Supermarket in Jersey that was known for their canned goods. You could get

10 cans of food for damn near $1.00. That was heaven for a person who enjoyed cooking or had a large family. Anyway, I always noticed as soon as we crossed the George Washington Bridge, the highway was a lot smoother. It almost felt like we were driving on air it was so smooth. Then we would pass these townhome communities and different neighborhoods that I knew undoubtedly was different from where I grew up.

For some reason, I always kept my shopping trips to New Jersey in mind when I saved enough money to be on my own. I wasn't even singing then, or even old enough to have a job, but I saw me living in this area. I saw where I was going to live years before it happened. I became an adult and was finally able to get out on my own. New Jersey was peaceful, quiet, and plenty of places to park. It was also a perfect place to raise my kids. I wanted them to smell a different kind of air and attend a good school. I was so over the parking issues in my hometown and I couldn't stand NYC for that reason. Never a place to park and when there was parking it was almost $40 for 30 minutes—ridiculous! Let's not forget the parking on the street, waking up to move your car before 7am just to park your vehicle on the opposite side. That was just a mess. For that reason alone, I just wanted to get the hell out of there.

My realtor Susan worked and resided in one of the most expensive zip codes in New Jersey (Bergen County) which attracted some high-end clientele. Susan Perry was the go to person if you were of a certain status. And when I say "status", I don't just mean "famous ". The area was flooded with Judges,

Athletes, Music Artists, Doctors, Lawyers, Entrepreneurs, etc. You honestly couldn't live in Bergen County if you weren't making at least 100k a year or more. Although she worked with anybody who needed a place and could afford her, the high-profile clients hired her because she seemed to understand the kind of privacy that was needed with a public figure/professional lifestyle. I guess we were all asking for the same thing—peace, quiet and to be left the fuck alone lol. Therefore, you give her your budget and she'll find you the privacy of your life—and that she did.

There were several cities in Northern New Jersey that were prospects, but I wanted to stay closest to the George Washington Bridge. After seeing some of the most beautiful, star studded units, she sent me a property that was not only close to the bridge, but it was a gated community with a 24-hour security guard at the entrance. This was no toy cop security guy. He was an armed professional, and you weren't getting through that gate if you didn't look like your driver's license or didn't have a gate key. I called Susan right away and told her, "I have to go see this", and we did.

It was a two-bedroom two bath condominium located in the back of the property. I couldn't help but notice the luxury cars that were parked in the assigned parking spaces. Now, I'm curious as to what kind of people lived in this community. What the hell did these people do for a living? Were they like me, or was I living amongst some of the most notorious drug kingpins? Yes, I guess I was being a little judgmental, besides, my judgement was based on the cars I saw. Professional people don't usually have cars with 24-inch rims kitted out with the dark illegal tinted windows. That not only sounds like someone who wanted privacy, but someone who wanted the attention on the outside, but didn't want to be seen on the inside.

The two bedroom/two baths were both upstairs. The master bedroom was huge with its own bathroom and the kids and guests would share their bathroom in the upstairs hallway. I struggled with that for a minute, but I figured it wouldn't be a big deal since I wasn't the "have company type" anyway. I could care less if anyone comes to visit me or call me, and I'm the same to this day. In fact, the only person today that has an open-door policy is my grand baby. Everyone else must call and hope I answer. No hard feelings, I'd just rather be left alone, and when you're left alone no one can be in your business and gossip about you lol. Chile, I'm a whole mess, maybe one day that would change, but not today.

Thinking of my tour schedule and me just wanting some stability, I told Susan I would take the condo, but not until I found out if certain things were in the area. Being a single mother and having two young kids I needed to make sure the following were at least within a two-mile radius: a hospital, a supermarket, a shopping mall and a nice school. We didn't have Google back then or Yelp. We had to put in that work or look in the phone book. Susan confirmed I was okay, and the contracts were being prepared. I called my accountant at the time to give him all the information and he transferred the money I needed into my personal account. Yes, you heard right, I had to go through my "Power of Attorney" for my money, but that is a whole other chapter and God was still good.

I can't begin to tell you what it felt like getting the keys to my first place. Just having the money at nineteen years old to get an apartment was unheard of in my community. I was blessed beyond measure. There were times I'd just go to my empty apartment and just sit on the fully carpeted floors and cry in disbelief. I just couldn't believe I was about to move my kids and I in a beautiful place in a nice neighborhood. The joy I felt was unreal.

Although I was overjoyed, I felt as if I was leaving my old neighborhood behind (friends, family, etc.). The neighborhood that taught me how to be a soldier and birthed an experience in me that was so hard to let go. All the things I hated about NY, I started to miss them in the weirdest way. Most of all, I felt like I was leaving my Godmother Jet who was so content where she was. I didn't want to leave her in that rodent infested building while I'd be able to sleep on the floor in my new place if I wanted to. I had to convince myself that it was okay to do better, be better and move on. Parts of me wished that I could bring my whole block with me. But my life was different now, I was the same person with the same heart, but a much different objective. I had to do what was best for my two babies who depended on me.

When I finally moved in, my realtor would check on me from time to time to make sure my process was going smooth. The kids were enrolled in school and now it was time to get some furniture in this place. Looking for furniture was easy. I ended up going to this furniture store I use to pass on my way to school every morning on 167th street and Jerome Avenue. I don't know what it was about this furniture store, but I used to window shop every morning I went to school. They had these beautiful chandeliers that were sparkling so bright and pretty. But I had my eyes always on the bedroom sets and mattresses. I always wanted a huge wooden headboard with lots of little storage space. Keep in mind I was only in the 10th grade and had no idea what my life was going to be like. I just knew one day that I would be able to afford to get my own bed—and that time had come.

Now, what my realtor didn't tell me that I was living in the same community as rapper Biggie Smalls, Devante from Jodeci, NFL legend Rodney Hampton, and rap superstar Pepa (from Salt and Pepa) to name a few. This explained why all the cars were so kitted up and the traffic of women that would periodically stroll through my neighborhood at times. It was always a party—and sometimes my ass was a part of it lol.

# CHAPTER THIRTEEN

## *My Biggest Accomplishment*

After rescinding my suicide attempt in NYC, I came back home to Atlanta. I listened to my sister's voice when she said, "Just Come Home". I had absolutely nothing but a peace of mind, a few clothing items, and the new love that I had for myself. Although I never looked like my situation, I was still a little broken inside. It's amazing how we can make ourselves look like a million dollars on the outside, but on the inside, the blood running through your veins feels like it's drying up.

I was so happy to finally be back home with my family and even more excited to be reunited with my babies. I knew at that point I had my work laid out for me. I could do all things but fail. My sister was staying in Decatur, Ga. in she and her husband's first starter home. It wasn't one of the best neighborhoods in the area, but hey, everyone needs a place to live. That wasn't going to stop me from moving on and doing what I came back home to do. I was amped and excited, but once I got settled, something really strange happened—reality set in. It just hit me hard that I really had nothing! I had no more apartment, no car, no plan, no income, no nothing!

I would spend days in my sister's home sleeping while she and my brother-in-law got up and went to work every day. My mornings consisted of waking the kids up, fixing them breakfast, getting them dressed and seeing them off to school. I was so glad Atlanta had the yellow bus. It worked out perfect because I had no form of transportation to get them to school. It was just a mess, but not the end of the world. I remember sitting at the kitchen table alone just crying. Trying to figure out how I got to this point. How could a life that started out so good end up with so many rainy days? I had to figure something out quickly.

After a few months of just feeling sorry for myself, my sister was fed up. She was tired of seeing me in this funk and saw me slowly giving up on myself. It felt like I was losing the little life that I had left in me. For those closest to me would know that I don't stay down too long. I was the girl who used my comedic timing to talk shit in any way I could. I'd bring a laugh to any situation, but for some reason I didn't find anything funny. As far as my sister was concerned, the days of me sitting on the couch doing nothing was over! She aggressively told me to "Get up and do something with your life". "Stop sitting around watching the days go by. You have kids to take care of!" "Go get your G.E.D or something and go back to school," she said. It was something about that tone that pierced my soul. My kids were everything to me and they were my responsibility. I always made them proud and did what I had to do to take care of them and I wasn't going to stop now.

It was the moment of truth. The day had finally come where I would change my life and make the best out of what was to be my new life. There was something special about this day. For some reason I felt renewed and empowered. I felt like I ate a can of spinach and could take over the world. That was a good thing and it was a good day.

## Get your Life

My brother in law allowed me to drive his van to get some things done while the kids were in school. So, I decided to take my sisters advice and "Get my life". I made a few phone calls and located the closest GED program I could find. I called and made my appointment to come in and lo and behold, they had an opening that evening at 6pm. Full of excitement, I couldn't wait to tell my sister the good news. I drove to the location to register, which was not in one of the best areas in Decatur, Ga. No disrespect to the residents of that county, but I was scared to death. On top of that, it was predominantly African American and there was a big chance that someone would recognize me—which I didn't want to happen. That alone caused another issue.

Why did this bother me? I'm not sure, but the only thing I could come up with was the fact that this was new to me still. Although I was moving on towards my next, the reality of my current situation was still planted in my head. After registering, it was all good and I felt comfortable. I couldn't help but notice the older people that were in there doing the same thing. I didn't know their story, and they didn't know mine, but I knew we had one goal in common—to get a High School Diploma (GED).

After taking six classes in total, doing the worksheets and doing extra work studying from the GED workbook, I felt I was ready to go forth with the test. Part of me was like F**k it, what do I have to lose. But the heart of me was so intimidated because it's been so long since I even opened a textbook. Now, I know I've never been a student with bad grades even in High School, and I knew I had the ability to test well, but for some reason I was nervous about everything that I couldn't remember or never learned. My instructor was the nicest person I've ever met. He was a high yellow African American that reminded you of a southern talking version of Tom Joyner. It's not often you meet an educator who connected so well with his students, young and old, we were all treated the same. He walked me through the whole process and was so encouraging. Every time I took a pre-test, he'd grade my tests and say, "Girl you're ready to take this test".

I couldn't believe I was doing so good on my tests, especially since I damn near guessed a few of those answers lol. Whatever the case, my self-esteem went through the roof. I felt a confidence that I've never felt before in my life. My instructor was the first person in a long time to tell me I did something good. After a few more classes and tests, I was finally ready to take a shot at one of the five tests required by the state of Georgia to get your GED. Feeling confident, I told my teacher I wanted to not only take one test, but I was confident enough to take five tests in one day. My instructor looked at me and said, "Are you sure?" I said yes, let's do it.

It took me the whole damn school day to take all five tests. I was tired as hell when it was over and a little uncertain. My emotions were all over the place at this point. One minute I was confident and then I was nervous again. Is that normal? I guess so. Besides, I had nothing to lose shit everything was already gone. Everything but my piece of mind. What I counted on the most was the fact that this right here was all on me. I couldn't blame anyone but me if I didn't come out of this one.

Five days passed, and I have to say it was the longest five days ever. I couldn't wait to get to school to find out my results. I was anxious like a kid hearing the ice cream truck. When I got to school, I went to my class where my instructor met me at the door. He took me straight to the front office where he told the clerk my last name and she located my file. I asked my teacher to look because I was so nervous. It's not like the results were going to change, but in my head, if it turned out that I failed, he'd be the one to be let down first, not me. He looked at my paper and said, "Why were you worried?". At this point I'm ready to bite my whole damn finger off. I said in excitement, "what is it?". My teacher showed me the paper and all I saw was PASSED, PASSED, PASSED, PASSED, PASSED. I passed all five exams! To be exact, I was twelve points from getting a perfect score. For example, if the highest you can get was a five hundred, I had a four-eighty-eight. Not bad for a twenty-eight-year-old former superstar trying to get her life together. I was happy, proud, and on my way to rebuilding my life. This was one of the few times I can honestly say my mother would've been proud of me. I know this may seem like a small thing to most people, but of all the great things I've accomplished in life, earning my High School Diploma was bigger to me than any record I ever sold.

# CHAPTER FOURTEEN

## *Working Nine to Five*

"Welcome to USI Energy, LeAnne speaking, how can I help you"? This is the greeting you'd hear when you called my extension. Yes honey, Lelee from SWV took her life back and that meant getting a nine to five to pay some of these damn bills that my music industry money was no longer taking care of. I had to look past what used to be and look at my now, and my now said, put that pride aside and put your big girl drawers on. I would be lying if I said I didn't have reservations about my now.

Putting myself in a position to be judged, humiliated, teased and everything that could possibly happen to someone that just had all this worldly success: platinum records, successful tours, international fans, etc. I was now just like everybody else that looked up to me—a regular working-class citizen trying to figure it out once again. In an instant, I felt like a vulnerable teenager looking for a way out of this madness.

I didn't think that my new adjustment would be difficult because I've never felt like much of a star anyway. My personal life was always very regular and modest when I was making a few dollars anyway, but regardless of that, I thought I was in my own world, people who looked up to you always see a "Star", whether you're working a regular job or not. Eventually, I would become the conversation piece of the whole company.

USI Energy was a water billing meter company and I was hired through a friend of mine, Victoria, who was a member of my church at the time. Thank God for her hooking me up because I was really fucked up financially, and I had some shit to prove—not only to me, but for my babies. I had to prove to them that mommy can get us out of this funk by any means necessary. Being on stage with the girls was all I knew for a long time, but this was a new beginning for your girl, and I was on a good path. I had to do something because I was going nowhere fast. My funds were low and so was my self-esteem. I felt like failure had kicked me all in the ass, but I don't know why. I knew I was doing the right thing, but people have a way of making you feel low and unaccomplished whenever you have a setback. I'm really a strong girl at heart, but somehow, I allowed my circumstance to get the best of me. I literally made myself believe that having a nine to five was a terrible thing, especially after achieving so much success. Or was it even really success after all, because I never felt successful at all in music? I'll get into that a little later.

I was leaving New York City after being up there for the summer. My sister-in-law's husband who worked for Amtrak at the time was nice enough to put my kids and I on the train back to Atlanta. It was a long ride but very peaceful. The kids and I played games, talked, and it gave me some time to think about my next journey.

After Vic gave me the "hook up" interview, I was hired in less than thirty seconds lol. I can't lie, it felt so good signing all those dumb new hire employment papers. You know, the papers with all of your personal information on it and the W2 forms you fill out at the end. As crazy as it sounds, I was really pumped up. But the paper that really excited my ass at the time was the one that disclosed my start date and what I was getting paid.

As a new employee, my starting pay was $10 an hour. Yeah, I know that doesn't sound like a lot, but when you're in between blessings like I was, those little coins felt like I hit the jackpot. I would be working a full-time job at 40 hours a week, so the adding begins: 10x8 hours a day=80, 80x5 days a week=400, 400x4 weeks in a month=1600. My gross pay would be $1600 a month before taxes and after I claimed my two kids, I think I came home with a little over $1400 a month. I promise you, I had notebooks filled with scribble scrabble of numbers and bills I had to pay so that money was being put to good use. In my mind I started to get a little cloudy thinking about all the stuff I had to do at the time that this income possibly wouldn't cover. But me being the person I am, I can budget anything you give me.

9/11 had just happened, and it felt like everything in the world just stopped. Atlanta was already slow paced anyway at the time, but it seemed like everything was going in extra slow motion and the energy in the United States alone was weird. They closed office buildings, no one went to work, and the leasing industry was really slow. Nobody was leasing apartments or even cared about one. That wasn't a priority at the time for many people because many locals had family members in NYC that they were worried about and were waiting for answers. That ended up being a blessing for me at the time because I was desperate. With half ass credit and a down payment I was able to get a 2 bedroom/2 bath that was initially market rated at $1249.00, for only $569.00. That apartment complex was so desperate, they damn near gave me the keys the same day—and I took it lol. I was so happy and for the first time in a long time I felt like everything was starting to pull together—one task at a time. Chile, I was getting my shit together and it felt really good. On one hand, I was elated that I was offered such a great deal at this apartment complex, but I felt so bad that so many people were mourning the loss of family members and friends as a result of the 9/11 terrorist attacks.

I had gotten used to my new life and what it had to offer me. I succeeded at meeting my personal goals and now I was just living my life the best way I could. I was a few years into my new job and for the most part very happy. I wasn't making the music industry money that I was used to, but I sure had a peace of mind. All I really had to worry about was getting to work every day and doing the best job I can so I could look forward to the bullshit .50 raise that everyone looked forward to every year. But what I couldn't get used to was the public humiliation that I endured from some of my co-workers and their friends. Every time there was a new hire, I'd hear the person training them saying, "Do you know who that is". Before they could even get a good look at me, she then goes on to say, "That's the girl from the group SWV". It was so frustrating having the life that I was working so hard to get rid of constantly being thrown in my face.

# CHAPTER FIFTEEN

## Mr. Tongue

I was nineteen years old when I met the most beautiful young man I had ever seen. He was chocolate in color, with the most beautiful big eyes and smelled like Saks Fifth Avenue. I can still smell the aroma from his cologne and Aveda oils he used to wear. I was new in the business, on top of my game, and SWV were selling lots of records. He was on his way to being the next big thing in Hollywood and all the girls knew that shit too. Honey, they were on him like white on rice, and at the same time, he was eating it up too—literally. I met him at an industry event, and we exchanged information. I know it was very crowded at that event, so I had no idea how we ended up exchanging information. All I remember was the SkyPager was the trendy form of communication at that time.

While at the event, I worked the room, shook some hands and took some pictures-- keeping my eyes straight on the exit door. I was tired as hell and ready to go, but not before I laid my eyes on this fine ass piece of a black man one more time. As I left, we made eye contact and he made a gesture for me to "not forget to call him". But all the while, when he did that he did something sexy with his lips. Back then, men licked their lips a lot for some reason. I guess everybody was on their LL COOL J shit lol. If it was cool with him it was cool with me. I loved every minute of it.

Just like a young girl in heat, I wanted him so bad. Me and Mr. Tongue finally got in touch with each other and we stayed on the phone for hours at a time. We couldn't get enough of each other. We talked about everything from family, entertainment, future goals, etc.; and of course, I eventually found out how much of a freak he was. Yes, he was on some new level freaky shit to be so young and he was sucking nineteen-year-old me right in with him. Mr. Tongue and I had more in common than I thought. We were the same sign, born the same month, were into performing arts and loved the gift of song. Music was everything! Although we pursued different entertainment paths, I believe in the beginning of our courtship, music was the real connection that brought us together—that's until we found each other sexually.

Believe it or not, but I was really shy when it came to sex. Although I had a few experiences, I still felt like I didn't know what I was doing. In fact, prior to this situation I don't think I had a connection with the men I was previously with. I'm not proud of it at all, but I have to call it like it was—it was honestly just meaningless sex. You know that "just because" sex. But this time it was different, I was already in love with this guy from the first couple times I saw him. I'm talking about that kind of love that made me think we made love already. Now, you must remember, at nineteen years old, I'm sure every teenage girl who was sexually active at that time felt that giving yourself to a guy made you feel special. We thought that we were good if we gave a guy what he wanted, and if it was good, you'd be around a long ass time. Yeah, umm hmmm just keep reading.

The site of Mr. Tongue just made me so excited. Being in his presence and knowing the way he licked his lips the first day we met, I knew he loved a good face bath. If you have no idea what that means, I suggest you keep on living a little lol. I never thought I'd ever meet someone that I could completely be honest with about everything I was thinking. From my life on the road to my sexual desires. He was my ear to listen. He made me feel that my worst thoughts were okay. I mean I damn near told him everything I was thinking, and I can honestly say, he was a young man with really good advice. Everything I shared with him he always talked me into the right direction. This for me, even at nineteen years old, was so damn sexy. An attractive man always looks so much better when he's smart and ambitious.

Mr. Tongue was the first person I told about me being sexually violated by my Uncle Bill's wife (Aunt Elsie). Of course, just like anyone else, he felt bad about me being violated so young, but he sure understood that I was now a whole grown ass young woman and I was a little experienced. Mr. Tongue would take that experience to a whole other level. After enjoying each other's company for a while, somehow all that talking on the phone brought us closer and closer together. We really just had a cool ass relationship. I think in the beginning he just looked at me like one of the homies, but I was plotting on him the whole time. I wanted to be more than a homie, lover, friend. After a while our friendship slowly turned into something more. We decided to give our relationship a try. I guess you can say we were now exclusive—at least that's what the hell I thought.

Being a brand-new artist and a little attractive, I was getting many requests to go on dates with some of the who's who in the industry. Petitions for me to accompany some of the biggest stars to red carpet events through my publicist at my record label at the time was the norm back then—but I was very focused at that time. I couldn't even look at another man. Mr. Tongue was everything I thought I ever needed at that time, or I was just strung the fuck out. I guess it was a little of both because I wasn't letting go. You know it's bad when you get sprung on a man before he even gets the cookies lol. Oh well, I didn't give a damn. He was mine and I was his. We were exclusive dammit and I had a boyfriend! They always say a woman knows who she's going to give herself to the first time she meets them. This is so true. I couldn't wait to finally throw this good shit on him.

I was living in Teaneck, NJ at the time in my first apartment, and he lived in South Jersey. Having two small kids, my home environment wasn't all that private most of the time. Mommy this, mommy that! I couldn't escape the demands of my two kids, and besides, I didn't want to expose my children to him just yet. This was a new thing and I was all-in and wanted to give him the time that he needed getting to know me. I felt more comfortable going to Mr. Tongue's Bachelor pad. The first time I went to his house, I could tell in every way that a man lived there. He stayed in a loft apartment and it was sexy as hell. He was by far the cleanest, neatest young man I had ever met. His clothes were in place and his shoes stood next to each other at attention. The bathroom was immaculate and the aroma from his apartment you could smell two floors down. I didn't know about him, but I was preparing myself for a good night. The whole night I was saying to myself, damn if everything was in place in his apartment, I was excited to see what his body smelled like. Well at least the parts of his body I couldn't see yet.

Every minute that went by all of my boldness started to go out the window. I found myself starting to get weak in my knees literally. I wasn't sure if I was having second thoughts about what I knew was about to happen, or the desire was bigger than the act itself. Was I emotionally ready for this?

Mr. Tongue and I had sex and it was beautiful. Being so young I had no idea what making love was, but if it felt anything like what just happened, I wanted to have that experience again and again.

# CHAPTER SIXTEEN

## *I Bust the Windows Out His Car*

I met my radio lover during a promo stop for one of our albums we were promoting. He was the coolest guy, funny as hell and just very smart. I was so impressed at how many jobs he held down at one time. I mean he had his hand in every damn thing in entertainment. What Steve Harvey is doing now, my radio lover was that and more. He and his partner in crime were the two black faces that white radio and television loved. He was doing his thing.

As time went by, I would run into my radio lover at SWV's double platinum party in Manhattan that he was hosting. Everybody was there and it was so much fun. I really couldn't believe three girls from Brooklyn, and Bronx, NY sold two million albums. That was a milestone for any artist who didn't really have the big popular machine behind them. Don't get me wrong, our label RCA wasn't the most popular label at that time, but they matched the popular labels with budget. We had money to do the same things that the popular labels did, so they weren't by any means a bullshit label, and besides, we had "The King" on our team—Elvis himself.

This celebration was really memorable for me because my mother, and my Godmother Jet was there to help me celebrate. This was around the time my mother's health began to deteriorate, and she started to slowly decline. I remember earlier that day as we were preparing for the big event, mom and I had a whole "Girls Day". We got our feet done, manicures, went shopping, etc.

We also went to every beauty supply store to try on wigs but had such a hard time. Mommy didn't really like any of the wigs, so I had to pull a few tricks out the bag. I end up getting my popular ponytail hairpiece I use to always wear at the time and told my mother, "Mommy you're going to look like me today". She said laughing, "Oh Lord, ok baby". After that she was good money.

My radio lover and I would keep in touch after exchanging numbers at the party. We were just friends having friendly conversations about the shit that was going on in the world of entertainment, as well as personal things we were going through in our lives at that time. We were both in relationships, I was going through my on again, off again bullshit with Mr. Tongue, and he was definitely that ear for me when I needed it. I don't know what it is about these men who have the best advice for people, but never take their own advice. I believe he was all over the place at the time with women. He was successful, older, and he appeared to have had his shit together. I'd be lying if I said he didn't have anything to offer because he was that and more.

The more we conversed on the phone, the closer we began to get. My relationship with Mr. Tongue deteriorated quicker than my mother's health, and we were completely done. I got tired of the emotional roller coaster I was going through after hearing about places he was putting his penis. I was done and my radio guy was there for me every step of the way. Every time I would tell him something I found out about my ex, he would feel so sorry for me, saying, "Damn, why he do you like that", or "You're such a sweet girl, I would do you right if you was with me". I let all of this marinate in my head and I never forgot it. Even though he was my friend, I started to find myself needing him more and more. I looked forward to the things he used to say to me and the wisdom he had just being an older gentleman. He was about ten years older than me and I've never really dated a man that much older, but this felt like it was probably going to be my first.

I must admit, the whole time we were conversing on the phone, and he was telling me all that good shit., you know being very complimentary and all, I had already envisioned us in a relationship. I saw him in my life some kind of way and lo and behold, it took a few months and he asked me to be his girl. I was a little shocked, but I was young, happy and trying to get over this damn ex-boyfriend of mine. They always say the best way to get over an ex is to get a new boo. I'm not going to say that was the best solution to my problem, but having someone there really helped a lot.

I was at the top of my game at this time and so was he. We were a pretty popular couple and I can honestly say that we complimented each other. Whenever we would go out together to each other's events, we would always acknowledge each other. At the time he was the most sought-after host and had one of the biggest morning shows in New York City. He was "The Breakfast Club" before "The Breakfast Club". I can recall one time where he had to speak at a school in Brooklyn, NY and I was there to support him, just as a good girlfriend should. It was so early in the morning and anyone who knows me knows that I cannot stand early mornings, but I was up bright and early to support my man and was very proud of it. As we pulled up to the school the staff greeted us at the car and proceeded to seat us in the auditorium. As my radio lover got up to speak after a strong reading of bio by one of the faculty, he graciously took the mic and thanked the school for the invite. Without me having a clue, he said, "I'd also like to thank my girlfriend who's here to support me, you know her, Lelee from SWV". I felt like I was winning an award. I graciously stood up and waved my hand to the crowd and blew a kiss at my boo. It really felt good that the day was not about me, but about him. He did a great job giving his speech.

From the moment my radio guy and I made our relationship official, I can't exactly say that everyone was accepting of our decision. Some of my peers thought I was making a big mistake, thinking I could do a lot better. I was young, fresh, making my own money, etc. Considering who I could've been with, they thought I was dating down even though financially, his ass was doing way better than me. Yeah, I was doing my thing and had some notoriety, but his streams of income were endless. Therefore, he was all over the place. And, I can't imagine what the trolls of women on his end thought about us being together, which eventually became problematic in our relationship.

As our relationship started to grow, so did our work schedule, therefore my personal time with my boyfriend was very important. I tried to spend as much time as possible with him whenever we had a day or two off. Even though we were living a few counties away from each other, I would often spend most of my time at his apartment, which meant I was exposed to a lot of the bullshit that would eventually ruin our relationship. I was never the type of girl to look through your shit, rambling, and going through pant pockets looking for the things that women looked for. I always believed that if there was something that I needed to find out, it would fall right in my lap. There were times women would call the house and I would answer. If he was home, I'd gladly give him the phone, if he wasn't, I would take a message, never once questioning the nature of their call. I knew the business he was in and I knew he had many female associates in the business.

Around nineteen ninety-three, ninety-four, my mom really started to get sick, so I was going back and forth from New

Jersey to Atlanta where she was in and out of the hospital. There were times when I would stay a lot longer than I planned to take care of my mom, but I would come back when I could. There was one time I came back and I was so happy to finally be spending time with my boo, I had missed him terribly. All the talking on the phone just wasn't getting it. See back then we didn't have the internet and Facetime unfortunately. It was letters, SkyPager's, home phones and nosey niggas reporting shit. They were our Mediatakeout back in the day. I would have to pass his house from the airport, so I'd just go straight there and stay a few nights.

On this night, as I walked in the house, it just felt different. It used to smell like me, I would have things arranged a certain way and it was changed. Not thinking anything of it, I figured he had a housekeeper come and straighten up a lil bit because I know he really didn't have the time. I just kept on being excited about seeing my boo. Of course, he wasn't there, which was cool because it would give me some time to freshen up a little bit and relax after the long ride.

About twenty minutes after I laid down, the phone rang. It was about ten something at night and I was exhausted. I didn't recognize the name on the caller ID, so I figure it wasn't important. Whoever it was could leave a message. After the third ring, something told me to answer the phone:

**Me**: Hello

**Caller**: Um, hi, can I speak to the radio guy?

**Me:** Oh, he's not here at the moment, can I tell him who's calling?

**Caller:** *Click*

The bitch hung up on me. From that point on, I felt that something was going on. I was so upset, but too tired to call him to address it, so I waited until he got home. The next morning, I woke him up and told him what happened. Of course, he was a little upset but swore up and down that he had no idea who that could be. I made it very clear that I wasn't going through this shit and to be honest, she sounded like someone who was used to him picking up the phone. Whoever this was, she was used to calling all time of night. I really didn't give it that much airtime because it wasn't like we exchanged any real words, but it wasn't the most comfortable feeling either. I addressed it to my boyfriend and left it alone. I'm sure his ass called her and told whoever he thought it was that I was in town. For a minute I thought about all the crap I went through in my last relationship. I just felt something was about to happen.

Of course, when me and my boyfriend spent time together it was always a ton of fun. The next few days, we had dinner and made our rounds through the city and beyond. I'd go with him to work sometimes and we'd go visit his family in Queens whom I still love to this day. There was never a dull moment because his friends were a lot of fun. They laughed, joked, and were a real strong support system for him. I could tell he got his sense of humor from his mom who has always showed me love. Just a sweet lady who can cook her tail off. She will always and forever be ma to me.

After dinner one night, he decided he and his boys would go to the strip club. I chose not to go because I was too damn tired. So, I went to the house and did my normal, take a shower and lay it down. The phone rang and I answered on the first ring because I was literally right next to it:

**Me**: Hello

**Caller**: Hi may I speak to the radio guy

**Me**: He's not here, may I ask who's calling

**Caller**: Don't worry about it, he knows who it is

**Me**: Well I don't

**Caller**: Don't worry about it, just know you only temporary bitch

I couldn't even breathe. My blood was boiling like hell. My antennas are all the way up and I was pissed. What was so strange was that it seemed like she would call when she knew I was alone. That was a red flag right there. With this call, I was convinced he had something going on. I couldn't believe the disrespect she had towards me. This chic was trying to send me a message.

The next morning, on my way to the airport I changed the phone number. I received a call from my sister Jeanette to tell me that my mom was back in the hospital. She was taking a turn for the worst. My heart couldn't take too many beatings at once, so I chose to focus on what I thought was more important—my mother. I got to Atlanta just before rush hour and went straight to the hospital. My mom was in the hospital after having a stroke and just couldn't recover from it. My mommy would eventually pass away and now I had a new set of problems.

The next time I would see the Radio Guy was the night of my mother's wake. We were in the hotel and I told him and was very clear, "If you don't want this relationship, let me go", I said. "No baby I want this, I want us to be together. I'm going to take care of you," he said. This is what he tells me the night before I buried my mother. He told me, he told my family, and he even told my father. Everyone in my family loved him and believed him. He was very convincing, until I put my mother in the ground and he went back home without me.

After doing those shows and spending time with my mother and family, I was missing my other half. I was gone for almost two weeks from him and needed a real strong hug. So, I called my boyfriend and said:

**Me**: Hey babe, how are you

**The Radio guy**: Hey Lee, wassup

**Me**: I miss you, I have four days off I'm coming to see you

**The Radio Guy**: (Pausing) Lee I have something to tell you

**Me**: Ok babe what's up

**The Radio Guy**: (Pauses again) Lee I didn't mean to hurt you

**Me**: Huh, babe what are you talking about

**The Radio Guy**: Lee, Kenya is back

**Me**: Kenya is back, what does that mean, I'm lost

**The Radio Guy**: I didn't mean to hurt you (sounding like he's crying)

**Me**: Tell me what's going on

I could hear a voice next to him, basically coaching him saying, "Tell her".

**The Radio Guy:** Me and Kenya got back together Lee

I quickly hung up the phone and got on the next flight to Newark. That was the longest 2 ½ hour plane ride I had ever taken. My body was overheated, and I was pissed off, angry, sad, suicidal, violent, all kinda shit. How dare he do this shit to me. I really thought he was older, different, and knew what he wanted. I guess he did because it sure wasn't me. He was no different than the rest of the niggas he warned me about. All I could think about was dude, you couldn't wait at least til my mom was three weeks in the ground?

I rented a car from the airport, called my sister Bonita and picked her up. I called his mother crying my ass off and told her everything I was about to do. All she could do is cry with me and say, "Baby just be careful, I didn't raise my son to be no dog". I knew she didn't he was just an asshole. I was fuming while Bonita was scared as hell. I was driving that damn car like ninety miles per hour, way past the legal limit. We finally made it to his building where the doorman nicely let me through the gate without checking my ID. Shit, I was just his girlfriend two weeks ago. I gladly went to the parking lot where his custom Nissan Pathfinder truck was nicely parked with plenty of open space around it. I pulled my rental up right beside it and went to the trunk and took out the crowbar. My sister Bonita offered to do it, but she was too scary. She was trying to save me from a scandal. By the time she looked around to see who was looking we would've gotten caught.

I Just didn't give a damn. My mother was dead, my heart was broken, and his shit was about to break too—fuck his car I thought. I slowly bust the glass out the windows and beat that shit up like it was attacking me. I then went in my bag, took out box cutter and slowly walked around the vehicle like I was cutting ice. Visible signs of vandalism and I could care less. "Let's Go sis, let's go", Bonita said. I said ok, but I couldn't go without the car still being drivable, so I flatten all four tires and broke all his mirrors. When I finished with that car, it looked like it belonged in a junkyard.

I then drove to the airport and went back home to Atlanta. My phone was ringing like crazy. I refuse to answer any calls until I got home. My manager called me with the girls on the line, "What the fuck did you do Lelee", "He's looking for you". I was as calm as the blue skies, unbothered. Then his manager called me with lawyers on the phone telling me how much damage I did to his vehicle. I told them straight up, "Fuck that car, do you know how much damage he did to me"? My heart is broken!! That was the end of that conversation. Life happened as usual.

Because the whole industry found out about what happened I was ordered to stay twenty feet away from him. We were at the same events sometimes, so there had to be some kind of order. If he's reading this, Thank You for not pressing charges on me.

## Lessons Learned

The twenty something Lelee was a mess. I had no idea how to channel hurt and pain. This relationship damaged me so much I now became the girl on the phone. What she did to me, I wanted to do to other girls. Somebody was going to pay for what I couldn't repair—my heart. All of the signs were there from the beginning, I saw them and even acknowledged them, and it went over my head. I should've known he was a shitbag when I found a receipt for a fur coat, he bought her for Christmas and guess what he bought me—some perfume I didn't like.

Today, I think about that moment and I see how we could have both handled this differently. I was about twenty-two and he was thirty-three. I expected so much from him and he did to me what all the others did. I don't suggest handling a break-up this way. I didn't give myself time to process everything that took place, especially after just burying my mom. One thing is for sure, no one can steal any man from you. He's either going to want you or not. He allowed her access to our space and she took full advantage of his weakness. It didn't help that he ended up marrying the side chick and she got everything from him. God don't like ugly. Girlfriend, want the man who wants you back, and never bust the windows out of his car.

# CHAPTER SEVENTEEN

## *Broke and Broken*

The year was 1998, so much happened at this time. I hated my life and everything that was in it. Sisters With Voices had gone their separate ways and reality set in real quick. After paying the taxes on the "Love Don't Live Here Anymore" money that RCA gave me to end my contract with them, and some bills that were backed up, my light was dimming and my days were cut short. Many people who I thought were my friends, suddenly disappeared or only spoke to you long enough to find out you couldn't do anything for them because you were fucked up too; they were gone too. Even though the money was low for me, I always held on to the little residual money that came every quarter and kept that for my kids. Whenever I couldn't eat, I made sure they could. I always tried to make sure I had a cushion to take care of my kids.

Every dime I got my hands on, I tried to hold on to as long as I could. I can talk about it now, but trust me, it was a conversation piece that I avoided for a very long time. No one really knew what I was going through because I never looked like my circumstance. I still kept myself together, I kept my hair done, and would put makeup on to conceal not only the invisible scars on the outside, but on the inside to. I didn't want to look like myself because I was no help even to me. I felt helpless, and worthless and almost like a burden to everybody that cared about me. The friends that I did have, I love them til this day, but I really believe the residue from my situation was so draining that I lost them to new friends who just had their shit together.

I wandered around New York City as if I was a Zombie. I lost my identity and had no idea who I was anymore. I only knew what everybody else knew—Lelee. But that person was no longer me. Lelee, as they knew her was the happy, shit talker, that would never go anywhere without a smile on her face. She was the girl that made everyone's day. I became a slave to Lelee, and totally forgot all about the pretty little girl my mother gave birth to named LeAnne. LeAnne was a survivor before the fame. LeAnne was created with some strong bones and wisdom. I forgot that before I achieved a certain level of success with my group, that I was SOMEBODY. I allowed people to dictate my every movement and even sometimes my thoughts. I had no control over my finances or my life. Everything people said about me I started to believe. I was a loser, I had no talent, I was a whore, I was ugly, I was going to have a bunch of kids and be on welfare. I was broken, and no one recognized it, but me. I'd look at myself in the mirror and see the scariest person.

I was literally afraid of "ME". It got to the point where I would never look in a mirror when I walked past it. I didn't want to look at myself because I was so ashamed. I was angry at the world!

I was angry at the music Industry, my label and everyone who had anything to do with SWV. I regretted even having the vision to put this group together and wanting it to work. There were moments I had wished that I had finished High School, went to college, married some wack dude from the Bronx, have some babies and live a normal life. Anything was better than my life at that time. This fucked up life of mine's the life that everybody thought was so great. The sound of my group's name made me literally sick to the point that I wanted to sometimes throw up because I couldn't erase that part of my life.

Wanting to end it ALL!!

I was at the Marriott Marquis Hotel in Times Square. I got me a room for the night because I got tired of sleeping in my truck in Yankee Stadium Parking Lot. Yes, it's true. I would stay up wandering around the city killing time, waiting for the sun to rise so I could at least sleep through the morning instead of through the night. Although, I had slightly tinted windows, I would still sleep with one eye open and one eye closed. You never can be too careful in New York. To avoid the risk of me getting hurt, there were other times where I would go to the girl clubs where my friend Lisa was promoting a party, hoping to see someone I knew or meet someone, offer them a ride home, in exchange for some shelter. People would usually leave the club about two or three in the morning, so by the time a conversation took place, the sun would be peeking through the sky. I felt more comfortable doing it this way, instead of going with some guy that could possibly rape me. I was in survival mode for real. My only motive was to stay alive.

I went through this part of my journey pretty much by myself because of my pride. I didn't want people to know anything other than what they knew of me already. I sure didn't want my family to be worried and I wasn't going to tell my friends. My sister Gigi was so upset with me for not telling her I was even in New York, let alone in New York homeless. I didn't have to sleep in my car when she had a place for me right there. So, it wasn't like I didn't have any support from my family, but how could anybody help you if they don't know that you need help. I was the one everyone depended on most of the time. Not always financially, but I was the one that sort of had it together.

I decided that I no longer wanted to be a burden to anyone anymore. I was so fucking tired of people asking me, "so what are you doing now", "why did SWV break up?". I was so connected to that brand that killing myself was the only way out—literally. Since I didn't feel celebrated in life, the whole world can talk shit about me in death because I was checking out.

I had no more money to stay another night at the hotel. As I began to pack up my things to leave, a weird feeling came upon me. I started to feel a heaviness on my body and my heart. It was the same feeling that I felt one time when I felt a dark presence crushing me as I slept. It felt as if whatever it was that was suffocating me, was taking the life out of me. Suddenly, I started to cry as if it was a dark cloud over my head and my thoughts were no longer my thoughts. If I had never felt what the sunken place felt like, this was it. I had no idea where I was going after I shut this room door, and it didn't matter because I would be dead from an 11th floor drop.

I went outside in front of my door and sat on the floor in a fetal position crying controllably. I pulled out my phone and proceeded to call my sisters. This was going to be my last conversation with them. As I'm trying to dial the number I was shaking uncontrollably. The first number I dialed was my sister Maleia, and her phone went to voicemail. For some reason, I started to cry harder because I knew the end was coming near. I was really going to take the coward way out of this. The second phone call was to my sister Jeanette, who had my children in her care at the time. At this point I felt like my heart was about to stop. As the phone rang, someone picked it up at the second ring. It was my sisters voice crying hard as hell, saying "Come Home", "just come home sis". At this point, the both of us were balling over the phone uncontrollably. I didn't realize what was happening at this time, but it felt like something supernatural. I believe that God sent a calmness through my sister because I was done. I started to get my voice back, and slowly it felt like my storm was coming to an end. I was starting to get in my right mind and think logically.

I hung up the phone with my sister and walked back in the hotel room. I literally looked in the same mirror that I was running from all this time and began to love myself again. My body didn't feel heavy anymore and I started to cry light tears. I was crying out to God thanking him for covering me over whatever it was that was holding me bondage. I can't credit anyone else for this people, because I was seconds away from taking an eleven-story leap to my death. Once I forgave myself, accepted my current situation and took control over it, I began to get my life back. It was now time for me to get rid of everything that didn't bring peace in my life. If God blessed me once, he'll bless me again. But little did I know the blessing was the gift of life. To God be the Glory!

## Let It Go!!!

At the time, I had a brand new 1998 Ford Expedition. Back then my truck was the new thing out at Ford. I had just traded in the first car I ever bought –a white Ford Mustang convertible. I was so happy to get that truck. When things got bad, that truck always had my back. I moved half of my things out of the apartment in that truck. It would be my studio apartment when I was too ashamed to tell anybody my situation. I spent many nights in my Expedition, sleeping in an empty lot at Yankee Stadium. Too bad it didn't last that long. I went for about a year trying to hide that truck from the repo man, until one day I just got tired as hell. Tired of running and hiding something that didn't belong to me anyway. I was broke, disgusted and couldn't be trusted.

 I had already downsized from a nice 3-bedroom townhome in Atlanta to a 2-bedroom apt in the same subdivision. It still wasn't good enough, to be honest I felt like I put myself in a deeper hole. I had no idea things were so bad until I came home to check on the house and my electric had been cut off. As a result of that, my food in the refrigerator had spoiled, which left a terrible smell in the house. In fact, that was the reason I came home in the first place to check on the house. One of my nice Caucasian neighbors had the office do a welfare check to my apartment of fear my kids and I were in there dead because of the foul smell. It smelled like straight up death!

For the most part--we were okay-- but my kids' hamsters were stiff as hell—dead. All I could do is cry at that point. As reality set in, it felt like doomsday. On top of that, I had to tell my kids the hamsters they loved so much they were never going to see them again. I remember getting my kids them hamsters to distract them from what was going on at the time. It worked for a little while until I told them we had to move—Again. Just like when I was a teenager, I would get evicted for the first time as an adult. I was devastated! Finally, I'd come to the realization that my professional life and personal life was really going downhill and I was about to lose it all—literally.

So many thoughts went through my head in this trying time. All I could think of was all these rich men who were athletes, actors, and artists that I dated and was exposed to that I could've called for help, but I refused. Shit, I was a star. I was Lelee, a member of one of the best-selling girl groups of the nineties and I was on top of my game. I wasn't calling anybody. It would humiliate the hell out of me if they found out my current situation. Nevertheless, pride had me all in the anus. It was so much easier to smile and front in front of people and pretend just like most people do.

As for my Blue Ford Expedition, I anxiously got in my truck and drove it to the nearest Ford Dealership. I originally bought the car in Atlanta, but I was staying in Pennsylvania at the time. It was there, I called the nearest Ford Dealership and made an appointment as if I was trading in a vehicle. I was literally driving this car with no insurance and very little gas. But somehow, I was always able to cough up a few dollars here and there. I was taking a chance on going to jail and jamming myself up worse than I was. The nearest dealership was about thirty miles away. As long as I had enough gas to make it there, I was good.

Once I arrived and proceeded to walk towards the front door, a nice, well dressed gentleman greeted me with a "Hello". I said "hello" and asked to speak to a manager. He said, "Hello there, that would be me, how can I help you?". I said, "This may sound a little strange, and I'm not one hundred percent comfortable doing this. But, I'm here to give you back what belongs to you". He looked at me as if I was about to tell him I was about to surprise him with a love child or something lol.

"I don't understand", he said. Trying to hold back my tears, I was completely honest with him and told him that I was going through a financial hardship, and I was just slowly breaking myself down trying to keep something that didn't belong to me. "I can't afford this truck sir, and I'm tired of hiding it", I said. I explained to him how hard it was for me to do this and he said, "I understand" and asked me to come to his office. I told him I had to use the bathroom but went out another door and never came back. It's bad enough I had to take the train back to where I was going, but I didn't want to be reminded of what just happened.

## Lelee's Life Lessons

Can you imagine being so BROKEN spiritually that you just want to take it out on people who have no idea what you're going through. It was so unfair, but when you feel like you don't know how to wake up in the morning or how you're going to go to sleep at night—it's a game changer. I lacked self-worth, confidence, and completely lost my identity. I had anxiety attacks whenever I would see people who I felt would remember me or recognize me. When I tell you, I blamed everyone for all my troubles, please believe it. I hated the music industry and everything that it represented.

Everyone who knows my story will always ask me, "How did you get through this?". Most are never concerned about the light at the end of the tunnel itself, they're more concerned about the process. I guess I can understand that, especially since I avoided taking any recreational drugs. As far as I was concerned, drugs didn't get me in this, and I wasn't going to allow any controlled substance to take me out. I must be honest, there were times I was alone and couldn't stop thinking about my situation. I often thought of ways I could just take the emotional pain away. Instead of going in a direction that would make me worse, I prayed and re-directed my thoughts. Instead of me drowning myself in pity, I decided to figure out how to turn my situation around.

As a working mother in entertainment, I sacrificed so much being away from my kids. We like to feel like we're enjoying the fruits of our labor, occasionally. No one wants to work just to pay bills all the time because that's not living. But life happens and it's always a relief to give up all the things that don't belong to you, especially if it's causing you problems. I must be honest, the drive on the way to give up my car was the most hurtful thing in the world, but the moment I left that car dealership I felt a weight off my shoulders.

I was holding on to baggage that was causing me so much pain inside. That's a lot of our issues today—especially women. We feel obligated to hold on to people, and things that we know is literally making us sick, but we'd rather be sick than feel like we're not being loyal. I knew there was one thing coming in between my truck and I—MONEY. And realistically, I didn't have any.

Having this experience taught me a lot about myself. I allowed the people around me to indirectly control everything that would control my movement. Accountants, Lawyers, and Management was all one big team. A team that never benefited me at all. A team that was nowhere to be found when things got bad for me. A team that was all about what they could suck out of you and the greatness you were attached to. But who was to blame?

Being a teenager when I started, and working all the way through my young adult years, I had no knowledge of anything. I never knew anything about how business worked, and not one adult around me found the time to teach me. I felt very taken advantage of and learned a lesson that I would never forget. I didn't ask questions because I never knew what questions to ask. It took me the longest time to even realize that SWV was a business. Oh, I soon found out when I got stuck with an IRS bill bigger than any money, I ever made being on the road. It was a lesson well taught.

The lesson in this chapter for me was to always be in control of ME. Whatever documents (big or little), especially in a professional space, always protect everything that has your name attached to it. Business associates had access to accounts of mines they shouldn't have had. I literally had to call my accountant and ask for money as if I was on a stipend. I was afraid to challenge my superiors when I was the one paying them. Never be afraid to ask questions whenever you're uncertain of something. It doesn't matter how big or small it is. I don't care what level of intellect you display ALWAYS ask questions! and when you get an answer-- ask more questions.

And as things got better for me, it helped me to grow stronger in my faith that if God blessed me one time, He'd bless me again. Whether it's a relationship or material things. Sometimes the hardest thing to do is usually the best thing. You must Let Go!!

# CHAPTER EIGHTEEN

## *From the Mouth of Babes*
## (my daughter)

Dear Moms,
We love you so much! You have always been the strongest women we know. I have watched you and learned from you. We have grown together and girllll I must say that, "We" enjoy having you around now more than ever! Lol

**To my mother**: You always did the best you could mom. You weren't always perfect, but you did more for me and my brother, not really having much to work with. You were a baby with a baby trying to figure it all out—with little or no help or support from the fathers of your children. I know that couldn't have been easy.

**To the single moms of the world**: I have a few things that I would love to say to you guys as a daughter of a strong, resilient, single mom.

1. **WATCH OUT FOR YOUR KIDS CONSISTENTLY!**
   No matter what, the cold hard truth is **YOU CAN'T**

**TRUST EVERYONE.** Some brothers, uncles, stepdads, aunts, are not "normal" in the brain and are doing disgusting things with, and to your kids. I was violated twice while my mother believed I was in the care of a trusted adult because she had to work. This is in no way her fault, but probably could have been prevented if the adult she left me with didn't leave me with a teenager. Bad judgement on the part of the adult who's care I was left in.

2. **ASK ALOT OF QUESTIONS!** Some kids will tell you what is going on if you simply ask them! Ask your children did anyone touch them or make them feel uncomfortable. You will be surprised at some of the answers guaranteed. You never know you could be catching something early on. DONT BE THAT NAIVE PARENT. Everyone's a suspect until proven innocent in my book. In the words of the city girls PERIOD. LOL

3. **DONT BE SO HARD ON YOURSELF** - motherhood can't be easy but you are doing a fantastic job. There is no right or wrong way, just trial and error 😊.

4. **KIDS' FEELINGS MATTER** -don't be so quick to disregard kids' feelings. They are smart and intelligent and can feel crazy vibes from people also. You, being the "adult" in the situation isn't grounds enough to keep them safe from jerk perves.

5. **SHARE YOUR STORIES WITH YOUR KIDS** - even though my mom doesn't think I do, I listen to all of her

crazy stories as a guideline of what not to do, because she put her pride to the side and shared it. Some stories are funny, some are dangerous, but all are good learning experiences and can help shape your kids. It beats the old, "tell them nothing and let them figure it out blindly method. lol

# Chapter Nineteen

## Sista HottPampa

When life happens, you don't know how to deal with it sometimes. Often, the life-changing experience may not even have anything to do with anything you did, but you embrace it anyway. I went around a long time trying to find love that was never trying to find me. I have been blessed to travel the world and beyond, seen some great things, met some great people, made a few dollars, but none of it ever made me happy. Honestly, it never got me close. That joy that I've been looking for came the day I became a grandmother.

From the moment my son told me he and his girlfriend at the time were expecting, of course, I was a little concerned because of the state they were in at the time, but I was never worried. I knew when my grandbaby entered the world, she was going to be ok. Unfortunately, growing up, I never had the "grandmother," "grandfather" experience, which I struggle with to this day. I found myself always clinging to a boyfriend's mother, or nana to get a little bit of what I felt like I was missing. I didn't want my grandbaby to ever experience that with me.

I connected with SistaHottPampa from the time she was in her mother's womb, and when she was born-- forget it! I was in stupid love! Her existence made me feel renewed and gave me a fire that I lost, chasing the dream that damn near killed me.

My grandbaby is now five years old, and her love for me has never changed. It gets stronger and stronger as the days go by. It's so strong that she believes that I am her Superhero! Whenever mom and dad would get on her bad side, she calls grandma because she looks at me as the "fixer." She believes I am the one person that can save her from the world, and I love that. I don't ever want her to feel that I am not her Superhero. I am going to beat doors down that's impossible for anyone else. I am going to fight for her when everyone else takes the gloves off. Now, I don't condone violence, but when it comes to my Braelynn, ain't nobody safe—kids, adults, pets, parents, etc. lol.

On a serious note, after everything great that I've done in the eyes of people, I would give it all up to be happy. We must be careful about how we define success and happiness. Happiness for me was not for a moment but was something I felt that was never-ending. It was never money, fame, notoriety, a man, family, etc. because someone always controlled that. I can honestly say that the love I have for my grandbaby is the Agape love that God has for us.

At a time when I was giving up on what I believed living a good life should be, her existence made me not just want to be alive, but actually, live. I am no longer the lady with a heartbeat that wakes up every day, but I now chose to live my life on purpose. Because of her, I have a reason to be alive, I have a reason to climb, and I have a reason to go after everything that God has for me with my name on it. The things that used to upset me, don't bother me anymore, the people that prayed against me don't get a response from me anymore. I've come a long way, and although it took me forty years to find it, I can honestly say I know what real love feels like.

If I never sing another song, get on another tour bus, or if I die tomorrow, I will leave here knowing that someone loved me unconditionally while I was here--My grandbaby.

*"And if by chance that special place. That you've been dreaming of....Leads you to a lonely place....find your strength in love"*
—**George Benson,** The Greatest Love of All

# CHAPTER TWENTY

*Ladies of Soul*

## 2017 Lady of Soul Recipient

 The day we received the call from our manager telling us that BET wanted to make us the Soul Train 2017 Lady of Soul Recipients, we were overly excited. BET has been the staple that has connected all things African American for years and we were overjoyed. After being in this business for almost thirty years, nominated for the most prestigious award in music, The Grammy, amongst others, and never took anything home, we were ecstatic that they would choose us to receive this honor.

SWV has always been the group that wanted to inspire young girls and women who looked just like us. Never because we were perfect, but because we were going through the same issues that they were. We wanted them to learn from the very girls they saw when they looked out their window. We wanted to be the vessel that showed that even a diamond in the rough can be used. Sometimes I felt like we were too black, too hood, too tomboyish. But the beauty is we were always true to who we were and never changed. We may not have received the respect and the accolades that the others have, but at the end of the day when it's all over, and we're dead and gone, the world will definitely know that SWV was here.

## My Speech

I'd like to thank my homeboy, my peace, my comfort when no one else understands, my Lord and savior Jesus Christ.

Bear With me for a moment, we have 25 years of Thank You's to get through.

I wanna thank my family for their love and support for so long. My kids Margaret and Khiry, my inspiration. My mother and father in heaven. I know you'd be proud.

Thanks for a great beginning to our greatness and legacy: Maureen Singleton, Kenny Ortiz, Joe Galante, All-Star, Genard Parker, Mary Moore, Skip Miller (RIP), Donald Bowden, Cory Taylor, E-One, Lionel Martin, Ralph McDaniel's, Debra Lee and our BET family. Our fans and day ones, what would this be without you. We thank you so much.

I'd like to send some crazy love to my sisters in song, Taj and Coko for this journey (good and bad) and the legacy that we've created together.

To our manager, Mr. Brooke Payne I thank you so much for stressing the importance of hard work and being women of integrity and passion when it comes to our brand.

**Ladies and Gentlemen,**

**"It's the passion that drives an artist when there's no label, no followers, no one knows your name, no bookings.**

**It is those times you are your own audience.**

**Work your passion, because it is that moment of solitude that builds character and gratitude, and fortitude that prepares you for the Soul Train "Lady of Soul Award— Thank you so much."**

Thank you so much Pastor Jesse CurneyIII for helping me nail this speech.

# I AM
# Leanne "LeLee" Lyons